New and Selected Poems

ALSO BY FREDERICK FIERSTEIN

THE FAMILY HISTORY (a play, 1973)

SURVIVORS (poems, 1975)

MANHATTAN CARNIVAL (a long poem, 1981)

FATHERING (a lyric sequence, 1982)

EXPANSIVE POETRY: THE NEW NARRATIVE
AND THE NEW FORMALISM (ed. anthology, 1989)

FALLOUT (poems, 2008)

DARK ENERGY (poems, 2013)

New and Selected Poems

Frederick Feirstein

Story Line Press | *Pasadena, CA*

New and Selected Poems
Copyright © 1998, 2021 by Frederick Feirstein
All Rights Reserved

No part of this book may be used or reproduced in any manner whatsoever without the prior written permission of both the publisher and the copyright owner.

ISBN 978-1-58654-076-0 (tradepaper)
  978-1-58654-095-1 (casebound)

The National Endowment for the Arts, the Los Angeles County Arts Commission, the Ahmanson Foundation, the Dwight Stuart Youth Fund, the Max Factor Family Foundation, the Pasadena Tournament of Roses Foundation, the Pasadena Arts & Culture Commission and the City of Pasadena Cultural Affairs Division, the City of Los Angeles Department of Cultural Affairs, the Audrey & Sydney Irmas Charitable Foundation, the Kinder Morgan Foundation, the Meta & George Rosenberg Foundation, the Allergan Foundation, the Riordan Foundation, Amazon Literary Partnership, and the Mara W. Breech Foundation partially support Red Hen Press.

Second Edition
Published by Story Line Press
an imprint of Red Hen Press
www.redhen.org

Acknowledgments

The author wishes to acknowledge the help of the late Stanley Lewis and Lou Kannenstine for publishing *Survivors* and *Manhattan Carnival* in a time when no one else would touch the dramatic or narrative poems of a young poets; also, the Guggenheim Foundation for having the foresight and daring to support the writing of *Manhattan Carnival*, a book-length poem of couplets. Most of all, he would like to thank Renee and Theodore Weiss for publishing the book-length "Family History" and the sequences of *Ending the Twentieth Century*, and Robert McDowell of Story Line Press for Publishing *City Life*, in which the verse play "The Psychiatrist at the Cocktail Party" appears. He would also like to thank Phil Zuckerman and Applewood Press for printing the lyric sequence "Fathering," *The Formalist*, *Edge City Review*, and *Atlanta Review* for printing the new poems "Hurricane," "Highway of Cheap Love," and "Childhood's End," and Claudia Annis for carefully typing the manuscript.

*For Theodore and Renee Weiss,
and Linda and David as always.*

Contents

from Survivors *(1974)*

    Walking Away   3

    "Grandfather" in Winter   5

    Edge   7

    Grandpa Borea   8

    Katherine's Broom   10

    Elegy   11

    The Promise   12

    A Luncheonette in Northern Maine   13

    The Film-Maker to His Father   14

    The Boarder   15

    Plumber   17

    The Hero   19

    The Widow   20

    His Halting Walk   21

    The Witch   22

from Manhattan Carnival: A Dramatic Monologue *(1981)*

    The Street   29

    The Blind Man   31

    A Girl   33

    The Crash   35

    The Stanhope   36

    The Child   38

    The Garbage Drummer   41

    The Jeweler   43

    The Windows   45
    The Meeting   47
    The Zoo   49
    The Jukebox   51

from Fathering *(1982)*
    Hospital   55
    Kaddish   56
    A Message   57
    For David, in the Middle of the 21ˢᵗ Century   58
    A Month Later   59
    Connections   60
    Foxtrots   61
    Unveiling   62
    Artificial Light   63
    Walk   64

from Family History *(1986)*
    Part I   67

from City Life *(1991)*
    "The Shawl"   89
        1. *Siddhartha Dove*   89
        2. *The Eyes*   91
        3. *Belle's Café*   94
        4. *The Grandson*   95
    from "The Psychiatrist At The Cocktail Party: A Verse Play   98
        Larry Corners the Psychiatrist   98
        To Larry Who Doubts He Should Marry   101
        Larry's Mother   102
        Joyce   103
        Renee's Husband   105
        Renee's Dance Partner   107

The Old Maid 109
The Guest Of Honor 111

from Ending the Twentieth Century *(1995)*

from Manhattan Elegy: A Sequence 117
    Manhattan Elegy 117
    Spring 118
    The Magic Kingdom 118
    Parade 119
    Spectacle 120
    Tell Me a Story 120
    Celebrating 122
    Underground Song 127
    The Sundial 128
    Song of the Suburbs 129
    Earth Angel 130
    The Poet to His Younger Self 131
    The Lake 132
    Journal of the Plague Year 132
    A Letter to Friends 133
    Fin de Siècle 134
from Creature of History: A Sequence 136
    Daydreaming 136
    Gravedona 136
    The Seduction at Villa Carlotta 138
    Stresa—the Borromeo Islands 138
    The Coup 140
    Venice Spontaneous 142
    Peasant Carts 143
    Trümmelbach 144
    Creature of History 145
    Survivor 146
    Hawaii—Drifting to the Volcano 147

from Time: New Poems

Hurricane   153
Highway of Cheap Love   154
Escape   157
Mosiac   159
   1. Jews   159
   2. *Go Down Moses*   *162*
   3. *Ethnic Cleanser*   *166*
   4. *Questions*   *167*
Twentieth Century   170
The House We Had to Sell   171
Childhood's End   172
Poolside Mozart   173
Blue Caribbean Picnic   174
Creation   175

from

Survivors

Walking Away

There were no cans or prayer books or dead dogs
Along the road, no snapshots or headstones,
No broken dolls, butts, newspapers—nothing.
Only a few memories troubled him,
And these he could suppress, he could.
And he could name the trees and sun and sky
And name the names: green, yellow, and pale blue
For the first time. And the sick or the mass dead?
Pine needles and the wet sun, the blue jay
Splashing among the branches, the Oz-green
Lichen on rocks: he was so curious,
Out of himself for the first time, since when?
There at the end of the road . . . the smell first,
He closed his eyes, of honeysuckle, yes,
Of thyme and bier roses and the man there
At the road's end, a bent-over harlequin
Singing an old song, old sentiments, yes:
Half-red his back half-green, half-red his hat
Half-green. Could such a private thing exist?
Oh, he would talk to him, become a boy,
Sit cross-legged at his feet and lose control.
The cold sweats began. The planes dove again,
The big guns . . . buttercups, spider webs,
The peacock green and stoplight red: keep still.
Still. Envy the white moth its folder wings,
The slimy things that Coleridge praised, praise them.
He did. And thought of poems: Four three two one . . .
Color drained from everything at once,
Except the clown, except the clown, the clown
Turned like a ball-turret gun upon his rock:
Rock upon rock, his buttocks: rocks, back: rock,
Head: rock. There was no more. His arms and legs

Were gone, as were the woods, as was the sun.
Nothing except the rubble's mystery,
Its quizzical last smile that was itself
An answer: "Did you expect a comedy?"

Grandfather" in Winter

The overcoats are gone from Central Park
—In the sudden Spring.
A clump of leaves, that lay in a white crypt
Of roots for months, loosens, looking for life.
Bare feet of hippies on the sunny walks,
Rock-heaps of pigeons bursting like corn, food
From brown bags, from white hands, from black hands,
Black and white kids kissing in the high rocks,
In the Rodin laps, in the hands of God
Above. Below, an old man, in a rough coat,
Wearing my grandfather's frown, lifts his face
Up to the sun and smiles smacking his lips.
His sky-blue Buchenwald tattoo has healed.
Below him, in the skating-rink, a small
Girl, Jewish, repeats the rings of the park:
The ring of her father skating around her,
The guard around him, the border of the rink
Around him, the rings of the pigeon-walks,
The rings of clouds, of jets, of the young
Sun around it. Me on the parapet,
The blood of the false Spring ringing my heart.
My wife beside me aims her camera at
The girl. The girl falls. The rope jerks. Nine
Iraqi Jews are falling through the air,
The Arab horde around them cheers. *Shema*.
The feet clump like leaves. The eyes turn up: white
Rocks. Israel in winter prepares again
For war. Around the gas-house are the guards,
Around the guards, pogroms: Deserts of dead,
Miles wide and miles thick. The rings around
Her borders are of time. Grandfather knows.
His dead eyes scrutinize my eyes. He knows

Tomorrow snow will fall like lead, the news
Will be obituaries, Kaddish will be sung.
It is the eve of war again:
Shema.

Edge

To set aside rage
And sit quietly at the water's edge
At the edge of yourself
And go past it
And live in the body of the duck
And the water lily
And the crumbs of your own gift of bread

Grandpa Borea

The siren's screaming in my head again.
This time it's Grandpa waiting to go down,
With his last preserves hooked up to his vein,
The sick king crumbling in his common gown.

Among the pots bubbling with grapes and plums
In his huge kitchen, we blow on tablespoons
Of juice, while Grandpa seals the vacuums
In the finished jars. Soon the afternoon

Acquires shadows, and our bluebird hands,
Heavy with cheese and *arancini*, close
Exhausted in our laps. Grandpa commands
His maid to bring us wine and dominoes

And we play silently, till night. We know
If Death should have to come, he'd be a friend
Of sorts: a fat boy, leaning on a hoe,
Life's spoiled natural son, who'd help him tend

His garden. Or a winter afternoon
In Grandpa's cellar, sunning among his lakes
Of wine and olive-hills, our flock of maroon
Fledglings perched on his shelf, eating steaks

He's broiled in spicy breading on a stove
Barbaric as a robber baron's smelter.
Some flood avulsed an ancient king's plush grove
Or roof-garden to make this luscious shelter.

We're on his porch, sipping anisette,
Watching a robin lift into the air

A worm at the peak of its pirouette.
He fits a perfect hand of solitaire.

And it's Spring. He makes his usual boast:
He's synchronized his aging with his trees'.
We feel his eighty-year-old heart and toast
His wisdom. Suddenly he's on his knees

On his cranked-up bed, Armageddon's come!
His leukocytes are smoking like jets
In the unnatural delirium
Of his metastasis. He can't quite get

The button of his buzzer to go in
Or his silly mouth to print the words
Of his sinking kingdom's final bulletins.
His fruit has turned to wax and his eyes to curds.
My head is screaming like a strangling bird's.

Katherine's Broom

Just for a moment, it is years ago.
We're kids again, we're giggling in bed
In winter, listening to the radio.

Downstairs Katherine screams, "Antonio!"
And swings her broom an inch above his head.
I punch the air and sing, *"Fortissimo!"*

The music stops and it begins to snow.
Katherine is in her kitchen, baking bread.
The streets are empty. We get dressed to go

Pounding down the wooden stairs *bravissimo*
And write, "We claim this town,
                              Linda and Fred."
Katherine reminds us that it's ten below

And the moment thaws. I hear the tiptoe
Of depression through my head
Again. I squeeze the wind out of my pillow

In rhythm with the dirty snow
Sweeping down the window. I leave the bed
Only once—to call the newlyweds,
Upstairs, to shut their thumping radio.

Elegy

He danced like a black bear to Strauss's waltz,
His lithe wife turning, turning on his arm,
In the circus of their sunny dining-room
That scarcely could contain his Russian charm.

He piled out plates with tired anecdotes
Of winter palaces and peasant carts,
Of gagging on his dog in time of siege.
He ate with a zest too heavy for his heart.

The snow could scarcely fill his mammoth tracks
Where his poodle shook off snowbells like a fool.
He loved the cold that wouldn't let him breathe
And sacked his stilted body for its fuel.

The Promise
(To the boy)

One day I'll return, on my old raft
The wind taking shape from my face
As water takes shape from a fish;
And on my chest your name
And your watch on my freckled wrist.

But promise when I come,
No talk of where I went
Or what I've done,
Or the self-despising fool
I've unintentionally
Become

Only of possible dreams,
No dreams: real water and sky,
And dances, and flowers, and fruit
—Where only the dreamless die.

A Luncheonette in Northern Maine

If the moose-head in this luncheonette could speak,
He would say, "Survival is all here."
But nothing here says much of anything,
Not since the Ice-Age: The native brain
No different from the mountain, the native thought
No different from the trees: indelicate, gruff.
Feelings? Blood warms, and the act of letting it:
The stuff these northerners are made of,
Men and women both. This waitress says
She hunts better than her old man or her son.
And who would doubt it, doubt her bashed-in skull,
Her half-a-mouth of teeth, her tortoise nails
Were not adapted to these witches' woods
Of frosts, of firs half-petrified, of slow
Jurassic nights, of barbs, of dropping cones, of burrs?

The Film-Maker to His Father

In every film I make,
Critics note an escape
From doctrine; time or place
Dissolves, frame after frame:
Moses casts his rod,
Becket damns his king,
Joseph bribes a guard,
Joan comes at the stake.
No matter what others take
For intellect, art; I know
That for each illusion I make
There is one scenario:
It's our unresolved debate
About where love must leave off
And how much freedom to take:
That's what my craft contains.

The Boarder

Stubborn Spring pushed through the cold twigs
In the small park across the street
From where Yud Schwartz, the poet, lived
With a deaf butcher and the butcher's wife
In one room cluttered as his grief:
Pictures of his dead wife on his desk
And of Schwartz, Sholem Aleichem and Sholem Asch—
Three cypresses on a Bronx street,
Two of them dead, Yud Schwartz
Cut down as well. His bookcase was
A crypt; his Yiddish tongue was dust;
And she dead a week—
Ruts for the skidding wheels of a Ford.

"How do I feel? I woke at dawn
In a yellow sweat, my sheets wet,
My guts wood, my head stuffed with grass,
With bluebird bones, fragments of poems.
I dressed. Buttoning my shirt was hard,
Believe me. 'There's one choice,' I said.
'Make up your mind!' and I half-walked
Down to the part. Forty-six steps—
I counted every one of them.
The clouds were rinsed of simile,
The sky bluer than Galilee.
The buds were out. I touched them: frail
As a wren's tongue, pale. The earth felt
Like bear's fur. Good, damn it, it's good.

"How do I feel?" He read a poem:
About wind, papers wrapped tight on his calves
As he walked Sholem Aleichem's streets, the old shops
Gone, slush soaking his shoes—gone poor,

Spanish in the tenement rooms
Where he spent the Sabbath afternoons
With his young wife, his poet-friends,
Peeled yellow apples and munched nuts,
Munched figs, and vowed to eat the world.

In fall I telephoned. "Who?" said the butcher's wife.
"The poet." "Who?" "The boarder!" "Dead.
Last Spring. He left no money and no clothes."

Plumber

He smacks the snow out of his hair: "Respect!"
His boots unclasped and flapping like a child's,
He kicks back in the hall to wipe them off.
"Six Fahrenheit!" Into his hand he coughs.
Then with a giant-step, he's in, erect.
"Plumber to play your pipes," he says and winks.
He played a flute once "that would drive girls wild."
"So what's wrong this time with your kitchen sink?"
"The toilet bowl won't work. I think it's stuffed."
"Use it for garbage, what do you expect?"
Before I can think of how to tease him back,
He drops to his knees, a candle snuffed.
I put a record on: Heifetz playing Brahms.
He exits from the bathroom, his eyes closed,
Hands closed, a choir boy humming psalms.
When the record ends, he blinks his dream away:
"You should have heard the way I used to play,"
He says and shakes his head until he smacks
His thigh to stop. "I used to practice five
Hours a day. At fourteen . . . Never mind."
He looks as his hand: "Thank God I'm alive."
I follow him in. He twists a monkey-wrench
In mock-flourish up in the air, then draws
It hard against a pipe like a fiddle-bow,
Then holds his nose: the playing or the stench?
He answers my look: "This was the cause,"
He shows his hand—deformed a little, scarred.
"The War. Poland. I used to practice hard.
When neighbors peered in the window, how I posed.
What do you do?"
                "Write."
                            "What?"

                              "Poems, novels, plays."
"Garbage, shit, they mix shit with art these days.
I used to see a movie or a show,
But now there's only violence, garbage, rape.
Who listens to Heifetz? Does anyone know,
These days, a way to help you feel? Or escape?"
With a thin, pipe-like tool he cranks, he finds
My toothbrush in the bowl. I look contrite.
"Look what you lost," he says. I nod, "Right, right."
He doesn't let me help him clean our mess.
I smile to let him see my helplessness.
"Who thought," he mumbles, "when I had my band . . . ?"
He puts away his tools. "Thanks," he says, "for that,"
Pointing to Heifetz, reaching for a hat
He doesn't have to tip. "If you want to flush,"
He says, "Don't fiddle with your brush,"
Then sees a subtler joke in what he's said,
Starts to extend, pulls back a dirty hand,
Then leaves backing out shaking, shaking his head.

The Hero

His parents take no credit for his fame.
Yet who but them created what remains
Of that frightened boy in their picture frame?
When he succeeded, he was ridiculed:
"His form was awkward" when he won at sports.
"He must have cheated" when he skipped in school.
But for his failures, he was comforted:
"It's not the winning but the fun you had."
And "Only misfits will do well in school."
And so he learned to cherish self-defeat,
To probe his wife for cancer when they touched,
To solve his business problems when he came,
And when he ate, food was potential shit.
His greatest pleasure was his children's game
Of hide-and-seek: he was always "It."
His business ventures always somehow failed
Either from moral niceties or luck.
Yet he died a hero when his train derailed.
His body cushioned someone when it struck.

The Widow

All night the widow races on a bike
Whose wheels are bolted to the bedroom floor.
Her husband's poodle naps against the door.
Her face is lifted, she has little scars
Behind her ears, her skin is like a child's.
But her hair is gray, and her gray eyes
Reveal a past that she won't recognize:
Her husband never called her by her name
But by the names he later gave his dog.
They slept in separate beds because she snored
And never talked because she had no brains.
And yet, "He was an angel when we met,
Before his business took his love away."
She only sees their good years, what he gave:
Candies, bouquets of flowers—even poems.
And now she has to live here all alone!
But she will give herself to no one else.
And so all night she races on a bike
And thinks of nothing but their early years:
How he was handsome, she was beautiful,
How he was strong and she was kind and neat,
How when they met "he swept me off my feet,"
How his job ruined them, how it ruined his heart
—But not hers, pumping like her legs, by God!

His Halting Walk

Did he sleepwalk here through twenty years
Of hopes chiseled, cheap miseries, fatigue?
For what? For whom? Not for him surely, yet
The chair was his, its tufts, its buttons: his,
The paneled ceiling: his. When did he choose
This lamp, table, this dish of jellied fruit,
Those children sleeping in that darkened room?
When did it start: the month, the exact date?

When he learned to write, he wrote his name this way.

The Witch

My right foot punctured by an iron hook,
I hop into the cab. I don't care
About the old woman that I overtook.
She hugs a shopping bag against the hood
To stop the driver: "Do you know the fare
To eighty-third and first?" I know I should
Offer to take her and to split the cost.
She looks poor, my house is close to hers.
But she looks like a witch whose path I crossed
In infant nightmares—her few teeth are hooks,
Her hair is iron gray or a cat's fur.
The driver turns, gives me a pitying look.
"I have to go to eighty-sixth and first,"
I say. "Let's split the fare."
       She squints, "How much?"
She winces, used to expecting the worst.
"Three bucks," I snap, impatient—I'm the witch:
My foot's too sore by now to even touch
And, having luck like hers, it's started to itch.
I back across the seat against the door.
It's hard for her to enter, she's so huge
She rocks, wriggles, until a kind of snore
Tells us she's in. She grins, her eyebrows raised
As if we were engaged in subterfuge
Against the kindly driver. I'm not fazed
I say by biting on my nail. We go.
"A dollar-fifty each?" she asks.
        "Yes, yes."
"I guessed it, so I ate no lunch."
         "Oh, no?"
As if rebuking me, my foot goes stiff.
"What brought you to St. Luke's?" I ask her.
         "Guess."

"A cold?" She shakes her head. "You wonder if
You're pregnant." She slaps my arm and smiles.
As if she's reading from a shopping list:
"Arthritis, slipped disc, sinus headache, piles."
—She can't stop—"Ulcers, in my left foot: gout,
And in the summer they removed a cyst
From here." She lifts her skirt. To stop her, I shout
"Wow!"
    "And dermatology: my scalp, the flu . . ."
I think in Brueghel laughter—"the Kermess"—
But only nod.
     "What's the matter with you?"
"Nothing," I say, thinking she's found me out.
She pinches me: "They make you, don't they, guess
Like they do with me . . . *You* have, hmn the gout."
I laugh, the driver laughs, and Falstaff roars
—Each tooth a victory for Hungry Life.
I set the scene: "Death on the bedroom floor . . ."
She squints. But not to see, I think, to hear.
"A pot-hanger with flattened hooks—my wife
Has left it there. We have just moved." Real fear
Is in her eyes. I want to stop.
      "Well? Well?"
I am her entertainment.
     "Fair is fair."
"I call a friend, hoping that he can tell
Me how to make our windows burglar-proof.
Especially in the back bedroom, where
A fire-escape sneaks down from the roof.
I go to check the window's height . . . Bare feet . . ."
She feeds on every detail with her eyes.
"And then I jump down from the window-seat."
My pain is in her eyes. She grabs my hand.
Her grip says: she wants me to sympathize
With—Morse code—her loneliness.
       "I understand,"
I squeeze back. "My wound knows. Only disease

Relieves the boredom of old age." She winks.
"They cut a twelve-pound tumor, of you please,
 From here"—she points—"and one from"—smiling—"Guess."
Each organ that she lists, she says "It stinks"
—False friends. Disease: true friends. The True Prince? Guess.
Her coat is torn in spots, her dress a rag.
She wears a man's white socks: "No one's . . . for the cold."
Her shoes are slippers, terry cloth. Her bag
Is stuffed with a chintz robe: "a dirty mess.
I'm on Medicaid," she says. "Now the old
Are taken care of—don't you think so?"
                               "Yes."
She lists the meager prices she would pay
For every operation, every pill:
Each one a victory, her eyes are gay,
Gay as I pay the driver for our fare
—No pride or thanks: it's from the common till
 That pays to thwart the burglar of our air.
The witch grins as I hop away: *Beware.*

from

Manhattan Carnival:
A Dramatic Monologue

Mark Stern Wakes Up

"Get up!" "Marlene?" I smell the April rain
And squint half-dreaming at the windowpane
Where winter light intensifies to Spring.
I pull the plug so our alarm won't ring,
Then prop myself up on our double bed
And dip to kiss the imprint of your head
And rub your pillow for Aladdin's lamp.
Oh, I'm a sheltered child away in camp!
Get up, she's gone, "Marriage is for the birds."
But who expresses feelings in *those* words?
Stockings, torn underpants litter the floor.
And who's that leering from our bedroom door?
Some empty-head I picked up in a bar.
Those words—*she* said last night and, "You're far
Gone, hubby. Nurse must bandage baby's heart."
But when she came, I smelled a silent fart."
    Tamed by ten years of marriage, I'm polite.
I cook for her so she can have "a bite"
Before she leaves to do her "nine to five"
And "Doesn't screwing make you feel alive?"
I want you now, I don't want a divorce.
Last night I rode a tourist buggy horse
Around the room where Pegasus once flew.
And infidelity? Of course, taboo.
I let her laughing blow my ear, "Goodbye,
You'll still be married on the day you die."
    I pace exhausted, though I slept last night.
I watch a jet plane's earnest gray goose flight
Between the roofs: from your apartment here?
I pull a tin ring off a can of beer
And aim the spray against a dirty pane.
Here's to you rain, more promising than rain!
Mark Stern's fizzled out... What's chirping? I rub

My finger till the window's clean. A shrub
Downstairs is budding—city warts but green.
Sun smears the ivy with a blinding sheen.
The super cranks her clothesline, conjuring
A flowering branch of colored cotton: Spring!
A blue jay leaves her husband's underwear
To soft-shoe through Manhattan's killing air:
A '20's dandy dressed in top hat, tails.
I rap the window with my fingernails,
But he is "on the town," the stupid thing.
This dying city is no place for Spring.
Or am I just emotionally weak?
I scratch the itchy stubble on my cheek
And dash into the bathroom where I piss
And shave and pick my scalp's psoriasis.
I shout into the mirror football cheers:
"You've lived on this stone island thirty years
And loved it for its faults; you are depressed.
Get out discover it again, get dressed."
  My eye is like a child's; the smog is pot.
Shining cratefuls of plum, peach, apricot
Are flung out of the fruit man's tiny store.
Behind the supermarket glass next door:
Landslides of grapefruit, orange, tangerine,
Persimmon, boysenberry, nectarine.
The florist tilts his giant crayon box
Of yellow roses, daffodils, and phlox.
A Disney sun breaks through, makes toys of trucks
And waddling movers look like Donald Ducks
And joke book captions out of storefront signs:
Cafe du Soir, Austrian Village, Wines.
Pedestrians in olive drabs and grays
Are startled by the sun's kinetic rays,
Then mottled into pointillistic patches.
The light turns green, cars passing hurl out snatches
Of rock-and-roll and Mozart and the weather.
The light turns red. Why aren't we together?

The Street

    The street is full of children off to school.
I enter them, swim in a wading pool.
She lugs a briefcase much too big for her.
He throws his hands up at a jabberer.
She beats her chest and howls like an ape.
He shifts his jacket to a Batman cape,
    And all those years we never had a child.
What books I wrote, anthologies compiled!
    I walk uphill—a hill!—a concrete maze
Conceals the roots of Spring where sheep might graze,
Where deer might nibble garlic from my hand
And lick the imprint of my wedding band,
Where we might find the time and ease to walk
Kissing, while neighbor cows and weasels gawk.
Maybe we'll walk across a stream on rocks,
Find fields of four-leaf clovers, poppycocks.
If we spent just one month without concrete,
Without the crowd's abrasion, in bare feet,
We'd be so bored, we'd learn to talk to ducks
—And they would say we were a pair of schmucks
To leave Manhattan Island as we know it.
Island? Thank God the concrete doesn't show it.
Instead we have our craziness and fights.
Our block with such cosmopolitan delights
That when we first moved in, I wouldn't go
To eat anywhere but in Mexico
Or France. What dance halls, beer halls, fast-food shops
—So wild at night each corner needs two cops.
Even that bank is lively with its flags,
Its jazz band sitting on heaped moneybags
That read *Grand Opening!* "With every new
Account you get a plastic kangaroo,

A yellow snot!" a dwarf is shouting. "Here's
Two plugs of free wax from an old man's ears!"
A group of bankers try to shut him up—
"A free electric... grnf... a porous cup.
Let go, you manikins, I'll bite your cocks!"
Then walks off, "Get your free, unnumbered clocks!"

The Blind Man

                                    "10-3-7 Lexington"
—A blind man, ivory cane outstretched, steps in.
His face is handsome with an English chin,
High cheekbones, chiseled nose, eyes marble-white
As if a bird had pecked them of their sight.
His coat is cashmere, Ivy League in cut.
He doesn't weave. He tries a cocky strut
Although the bus jerks out of the stop.
He smacks each hanger like a razor strop.
A woman stands and offers him her seat.
He quickly sits and pulls in dainty feet,
Then pulls an old man to his hearing aid:
"I would appreciate it if you paid
My fare. Is this eight nickels and a dime?'
The old man says, "Of course" in pantomime,
Then toddles forward, toddles slipping back.
And then the blind man opens his attack:
"My name is Paul D. Hartley-Robertson.
Excuse me but I talk to everyone
In buses, toilets, restaurants, and stores.
What work do you do?" Then—without a pause
To hear "A psychoanalyst"—"Oh, yes?
I knew it by your voice. Now you must guess
What job I work at, I am very rich.
My loneliness is like a maddening itch
That I can't scratch, that I can't even find.
The least part of my plight is being blind.
I'd like to phone you. I keep friends that way
Or visit you—at any time of day.
The friends I make in coffee shops or buses
Support my spirit by Bell's rupture trusses."
The old man smiles. The blind man pushes on:

"You'll never guess what I read in the john."
"Oh, *Playboy Magazine*."
                              "How did you guess?"
The old man purrs an analytic "Yes."
"They make too much of sex. Their jokes are great.
 Masters and Johnson I think deprecate
 The holy beauty in the act, don't you?
 Like children sticking pencils into glue."
The old man laughs, "I think, perhaps, you're right."
"To love is not to have an appetite
 For someone's organ like a slab of liver.
 Have you read *Portnoy*? God, it makes me shiver.
 In other words, no love, no sex.
 And you think what? This business is complex."
The old man bends, "Your stop on Lexington."
The blind man: "10-3-7 Robertson,
What's yours?" The old man, silent, pulls him up.
The blind man from his pocket pulls a cup
And smacks it in the old man's guarded face,
Then stumbles off, "You've *queered* another case."
The old man snorts, "A busman's holiday."
His face unmasked is coronary gray.

A Girl

    I'm starting at a girl with Chinese hair,
With harpist hands, skin white as a pear.
She's almost you when young. She wears your grace
—As if she's naked in a sheath of lace.
Her sitting still is actually the sum
Of all potential motion. If I come
To you, an older brother, take your hand,
Say when you're insecure I won't demand
You be less innocent than this young girl . . .
    The Seventies behind me in a whirl
Of barbershops and bakeries and banks.
The psychoanalyst leans back and yanks
The signal cord to stop. I'm in the bus
—This toughened Me is so preposterous—
Because I want to be where we began.
I rub my ring scar for a talisman,
Then slam the unlocked door and hurtle out
And, like the shrink, with his defeated pout,
The past's ahead of me—your favorite shops
Awaiting us. I haven't written flops,
You aren't terrified that we are poor,
You don't suggest my pen begin to whore
For advertising agencies and soaps
    Or scream, "We can't feed children on your hopes."
The world looks simple in these fancy blocks.
There are no grandmothers in army socks
With all their worldly goods in paper bags,
No windows warped or cracked and stuffed with rags.
Instead old mansions, churches, private schools,
And rooftop gardens, rooftop swimming pools.
This market selling jumbo squab and goose,
That florist selling miniature spruce,

This dress shop with its leftist magazines
And racks (here poor is chic) of faded jeans.
We squatted here, pitched pennies at the wall
And through that ladder hooked a basketball.
We bicycled and rowed in Central Park.
We necked, defying muggers, after dark.
We sauntered nibbling sauerkraut like grapes.
When maids or doormen sneered we swayed like apes.
We ran like blind men once for seven blocks,
Both stricken by a midnight urge for lox
And settled for a closing pizza stand
And once... Your life now? Mine seems second-hand.
I have to call you... calmly now... it's dead.
The slot is sealed off with a plug of lead.

The Crash

    I hear a crash and turn. A wall of flame
Surrounds a car. I'm hollering your name.
The passersby first freeze, then screaming run.
The burning car is like a loaded gun.
A doorman grabs my belt to hold me back,
"That woman"—Woman!—"must be charcoal black."
I shout, "The cab that hit her . . . over there!"
The doorman pleads, "He doesn't have a prayer!"
I pry the door. He's married to the wheel.
He doesn't look alive, I reach to feel
His pulse. "You nut, get out before it blows!"
The cabbie's life is ebbing from his nose.
"Exhaust pipe's catching fire, hurry up!"
I pull him free and make my palm a cup
To stop his bleeding. Someone hugs his feet.
We lug him way past safety down the street.
    I'm suddenly in Lenox Hill berserk,
Bellowing at an intern, "Hurry, jerk!"
A fire engine's siren tears the air,
Then hundred more—lunatics at their hair.
The cabbie's face has dribbled into gray.
I squirm from pats and handshakes, storm away.
I won't look back as hoses douse the pyre.
Remember how my greatest fear was fire?
And if I was a hero, would you love me?
At least, Marlene, you'd think much better of me.

The Stanhope

      My lungs are bruised, my ribs are tightened belts,
My eyes are cuts, my sinuses are welts.
I jog to heal them with sulfuric air.
I dodge a dog by leaping up a stair,
Then jitterbug past French and Parke-Bernet.
A woman cries in Bronxite, *"Je ne sais!"*
Another shouts, "Watch it, you'll still get old!"
The New World's paved with dog-shit, not with gold
And tasteless in its art. These galleries
Are filled with junk the touring Japanese
Cart home with moccasins, tin Empire States,
Key chains with footballs, paper license plates.
Let's try this phone. A punk's torn off the dial.
A cabbie greets me with a futile smile:
"There's nothing in this area that's straight.
The City Council sluts should get the gate.
Push-button phones: logical to install?
Instead they push a midtown shopper's mall
And ruin my business . . . " "Sorry, full of smoke,
I've got to run." "This Mayor is a joke!"
He shouts, loping beside me down the block.
"You want to suck a cabbie's twelve-inch cock?"
I pick up speed. I sprint. He falls behind
And panting rasps, "A priest once fucked my mind,
Then shot me naked with a movie lens."
I want to hear the pigeons, squirrels, wrens
—As natural as litter in the park.
I want to see a toy boat disembark
Imaginary insects from the pond
Who strut to Alice, hand poised like a wand.

I want to drink from fountains at the Met.
I want to nibble nuts, sip anisette

Together at The Stanhope's French Café
You painted, furred, me sporting a beret.
That was your fantasy, to sit like swells:
Primped, feminine, your thoughts all bagatelles
And me the waiter's tyrant, me John Wayne,
Me Tarzan, you—a Women's Libber—Jane.
     Why didn't I indulge you, play your mother?
Instead I ridiculed you, "Find another
Sugar-daddy. What 'Libber'? You're a kid."
I didn't know how true that was, you did.
A sixty-year old man in banker's clothes,
His veiny calves, I'm sure, in gartered hose
And in his buttonhole, each day, a rose.
We had an open marriage. My affair
Was with your twin: high cheekbones, long black hair
As all since then have been. That empty head
Last night was you. Does he still share your bed?
     You hear that infant howling, "Feed me, please?"
Your mother's in the kitchen on her knees
And praying to the Virgin for the strength
To discipline you, keep you at arm's length.
Your needs are sins; your kicking, flailing: crimes.
She'll feed you only at appointed times.
And me? My Momma cracked my Poppa's nuts,
Accused him hourly of "chasing sluts."
To keep her still, he decked her out in fur.
Gigantic diamonds, learned to worship her.
I vowed I'd never be a Jewish eunuch.
To nibble nuts here would have been my Munich.

The Child

    "Get natural Italian ices, cuz,"
A vendor shouts, "I'm licensed by the fuzz!"
Beside him a balloon man with a grey
Rocket of helium makes a bouquet
Of purple, orange, yellow, white, and pink.
The ices-man, "Get also orange drink!"
A tourist wearing giveaway white gloves,
A straw hat with a pin of turtle doves,
Asks for the flavors in a Southern drawl.
The ices-man snaps, "Just one left, that's all."
"A typical New Yorker," she replies.
Stunned by those words, tears welling in his eyes,
He lifts her hand and kisses it. "For you
—For free! dear lady, take my special brew."
She sucks a cup of all his remnants mixed.
A rainbow "Typical New York" has fixed.
She walks away perplexed: is this one mad?
He beams, "Two years an immigrant, not bad!"
But no one else will buy his rainbow ice.
    "Here's white balloons with little colored mice
Right in them, see?" "Mommy, oh please!" "Not now!"
"You always promise, but you never get."
"Sometimes, you know, a person must forget
His pleasures." "Why?" "Because you are a brat."
"What did I do?" "You've taken off your hat
To spite me." "But it's warming up, it's Spring!"
"You've disobeyed me, you can't have a thing."
"I'll keep it on for one balloon—a deal?"
"No bargains with the devil" "Pleeease!" "Pigs squeal."
She wrings her pocket for a cigarette.
"Society," I say, "will pay your debt
In violence." "What!" she screams, her ears blood-red.
"Don't spoil your child," I say. "Creepo? . . . Drop dead!"

I walk away. I want the child to follow.
And for a decade—why!—your womb was hollow.
    I lose myself in an uproarious crowd.
Although a sign reads, "No Feeding Allowed,"
A squat gorilla nonchalantly licks
A rainbow ice, and then to spice it up he picks
His nose—"Gorilla sprinkles!"—the crowd loves it,
Then twists the cup and through the mesh he shoves it.
"That means the ape wants more!" "Another cup!"
That mother runs to buy one, "Fill 'er up!"
And glares at me, triumphant. The crowd cheers
When, in their midst, torch high, she reappears.
    Above the ape house our native bird
The pigeon sits, too shocked to say a word.
The tiger weathervane turns frantically.
The wrens explode in an apostrophe.
The squirrels, suicidal, pace the cage.
The child in me, *my* child, berserk with rage
Buys all the white balloons and colored mice
And hands them to the child, "For being nice,"
And to the mother, "Let me buy this gift."
She glares triumphant once again. I drift
To where the parrots and macaws shriek color.
A keeper stirring coffee with a cruller
Says, "Saw that, pal. That woman's for the birds.
A month ago, the two of us had words.
This hand all on its own became a fist.
It took religious training to resist."
He shakes his crotch, "With this we'd make her learn
What kids are made of, huh?" I smile and turn
Away. A seal, a human amputee,
Suns on her back with a serenity
That turns her to a mermaid with a trunk
So sensual I'd want to fuck, if drunk
—Not drunk, I want my prick to be a tongue
Demanding flowers grow in this world's dung.
I want to fuck that giddy nine-year-old,

Her hair a sheet of Rumpelstiltskin gold.
That seal's mouth must be like a baby's cunt.
I want to make the female grizzly grunt
And watch the tigers in the darkness mate
And urge the baby gnu to masturbate
And kiss each waitress in the park café,
Then prance among the patrons, flagrantly gay.
Not even fantasies would we allow.
Why when we married did we make that vow
Of even thought-fidelity, Marlene?
To drive each other crazy was obscene.

The Garbage Drummer

      I try to find a clearing on a bench
Crowded with chattering Japanese and French,
And more are coming down the thoroughfare
From lobbies in The Plaza and Pierre.
A native shifts to make a spot for me.
I thank him but he's lost in melody,
Shaking his head, his eyes glazed, fingers popping.
Though he is sitting, he is Lindy-hopping.
His partner is a black attaché case.
He has a criminal, a killer face:
Low forehead, tiny ears, scarcely a chin,
Long greaseball hair, a leopard's hungry grin.
He wears a dirty white shirt, white silk tie,
Cufflinks of broken lapis lazuli.
His pants are pegged. He wears a cowboy belt;
A sort of sheath of brown rain-stiffened felt
Hangs from a loop. He eyes his watch, then booms
"It's Showtime!" But the tourists shrug and smile.
The thoroughfare becomes a nightclub aisle.
He overturns an empty garbage can.
A tourist shouts, "A New York hooligan!"
A cheer goes up. He takes it for applause,
Then lifts his hands high for the crowd to pause.
He lays his case upon the can—a drum.
He twirls his sticks and then sings out, "Ta Dum!
The style of that great genius Buddy Rich,
A style which I can imitate, but which
Cannot be stolen, it's a signature.
But study will transform the amateur
To this . . . " His sticks start rapping with such skill
I feel a '40's bobbysoxer's thrill.
I know his face. He was a famous man.
It's . . . who? reduced behind that garbage can.

"It's Krupa now. You recognize that beat?"
I'm clapping, shouting "Bravo" on my feet.
The stupid crowd is cheering with derision.
The drummer stops, "We'll have an intermission."
The sneering crowd throws coins. He picks them up
And humbly mutters, "I must get a cup."
"You're brilliant, man," I say, "So why this gig?"
"They catch you forging checks when you get big."
  He turns to beg. I realize he's me,
Childishly giving work away for free.
At first it seemed to suffer was romantic.
Who dreamt of being anxious, laughed at, frantic?
Or, fearing the imprisonment of work,
My father in his bank cage, petty clerk,
His moral dicta: *compromise and grin.*
A man is one who keeps his feelings in
Until he doesn't feel. Survive! Survive!
A man is one who seems to be alive.
The garbage drummer shouts, "You folks must pay
To keep my self-respect, or I won't play."
A Frenchman drops a coin, pinches his cheek.
Who cares for art? The drummer is a freak.
"I will not be an advertising whore!"
I wanted to be taken care of, poor
Enough to make my father right, a man!
We lived inside a mirrored garbage can.
Each day I grew more passive, you more wild.
The child is only father of the child.

The Jeweler

     I dash out where a thousand watches say
It's 4:15, you're thirty-five today.
Oh no, I'm all potential, I'm eighteen
And charming, carefree. Am I not, Marlene?
You see yon tray of jewels, my faithless Queen?
Shall one grace your pale bosom or your ear?
A jeweler crooks his finger, "Come in here.
I've got the lowest prices on the street.
I know what you want. This one's most discreet."
He holds a ruby pendant to the light.
"The treasure of an exiled Muscovite."
    I snort, he smiles—"A doctor, like my son."
"A what?" I ask. "Don't fake. I know it from
The hippie way you dress. It's your day off
I know, but I can't leave here and this cough . . ."
He opens up a mouth of onion soup.
"My day off, mister." "Does it look like croup?
I'll pay for diagnosis! What's your price?"
"That simple wedding band." "It's very nice."
"Could you inscribe it?" "Yes." "*Forever five . . .*"
"That's cute." " . . . *The only way to keep alive.*"
"I think you're a psychiatrist." "You're right."
"The grandson of an exiled Muscovite."
    I wince, he laughs—"The ring for one small peek,"
Then like a father slaps me on the cheek.
His tongue is ugly, geographical.
"Say *Ahh* . . . Your problem is—electrical."
"What's that!" he shouts. "You like the girls?" "Of course."
"Your wife?" "You ever see a milkman's horse?
—Except no milkman takes her off my hands."
"Did you once buy each other wedding bands?"
"I think all you psychiatrists are nuts."
"Your throat is sore from sticking in your putz."

"You mean the Clap?" he claps his forehead, "No!"
"I mean, too much can make resistance low."
 His eyes are panicked, wild birds in a cage.
 I realize your lover is his age.
"Doctor, how long must I abstain?" "A week."
 Relieved, he slaps me lightly on the cheek.
"I'll have your ring inscribed in half an hour.
 My wife, I used to call her 'City Flower.'"
 I leave him hands clasped, weeping at your ring.
 The traffic noise outside is deafening.

The Windows

      I need the windows of the Tourist Boards
On Fifth—their beaches, lower Alps, and fiords—
The students playing clarinet duets,
The mime in top silk hat and epaulets,
The Hari Krishnas spreading incense, joy,
Their flowing peach robes, shoes of corduroy,
The blind man singing hymns, St. Thomas Church,
The scaffolding where whistling workmen perch,
The haughty English manager of Cook's,
St. Patrick's nave, Rizzoli's picture books,
Tiffany's clock, the pools of Steuben glass,
The pocket park with cobblestones for grass.
Remember how we'd stroll on your lunch hour?
My nickname for you then was "City Flower."
      I turn towards Sixth, past two construction sites,
Through crowds. A girl in ballet shoes and tights
Pirouettes down the block, her raised hands moths.
"You want my stock of English terrycloths?"
"A smart guy puts his money in a bank."
"So when I told him that his foreplay stank . . ."
A drill starts up. "Big dildos, two bucks!" Where
Are you, Marlene? "He told me, '*You* are square!'"
The girl is in a swan's pose, lifted up.
The crowd applauds. The blind man shakes his cup,
Protesting joy. The crowd moves on. Marlene,
Are you somewhere in this Zanuck scene?
      Under this thin shattering crust of stone,
A train is roaring, "You must die alone."
But I can't live alone, with silent nights,
Without the heat and contact of our fights,
With anonymity, trapped in my time,
Communicating like a "glassed-in" mime.
The air is cut by helicopter blades

Above these glacial skyscrapers, cascades
Of workers, blue-faced, trapped at their machines.
I'd love to blow this block to smithereens,
Especially that emblem of our age
The Hotel Hilton, concentrate my rage
Upon one Building Trades conventioneer,
Give him a New York City souvenir.

The Meeting

      These lights are slow. I'm going to be late.
I still have Broadway's hordes to navigate.
Come on you red-eyed Cyclops, change! "Curse who?
I'm talking to the traffic light, not you."
"Stop thief!" a hooker tugs me, as I dart
Through pimps and Johns. If we are forced apart
By this old lady's poodle . . . "Sorry, wait
Till I catch my breath . . . You cut your hair? Looks great."
I want to ruffle it and say It's *me*
And stop this small-talk, this formality
Of gesture, tone of voice . . . "The Theater's dead
As usual." I want to take your head
Between my hands and touch your non-stop tongue
With mine—as on this New Year's Eve I hung
A mistletoe above your photograph
And kissed . . . I haven't heard that nervous laugh
For months. "Why did I call today? It's Spring!
Let's talk in there." (Damn, I forgot the ring!)
      This place is awful. Ceilings like a bank.
Enormous champagne bottles. And this swank
Wallpaper from the thirties! Even time
Is marketed these days. Jesus, now I'm
Chattering nervously—like our first date.
Waiter? We'll both have the roast beef hot plate
(Just as we had it then), coffee with cream . . .
I ordered without asking from a dream,
Not from my "piggish maleness." Oh Marlene,
Stop preaching. We're repeating our last scene:
You breathing hard from Libber's rage, not passion,
Me mocking my arch-enemy: Fashion.
Please, let's pretend we're not destroyed by time
Or social change. A man is in his prime
At thirty-five and, God, I feel half-dead,

Reduced by half, like our half-empty bed . . .
    I haven't slept around much—funny phrase—
Although it is like sleeping: sex, these days . . .
Thank God you left him! . . . How could I have guessed? . . .
You thought an open marriage suited *me*?
I lied to you to save some dignity! . . .
I've needed you no more than I need breath . . .
Of course I'm changing—quickly into death.
I need two children sucking at your tits.
'I need each mortal inch of you, your fits
Of baby-talking, bargain-hunting; fears
Of poorhouse, workhouse, welfare . . . I'm all ears.
Loneliness makes me blabber . . . I feel
That too about you, that you had to *steal*
Affection . . . Don't call yourself "a bourgeois bitch,
A hypocrite!" You needed something rich
To nourish you. I couldn't ease your hunger . . .
I don't know why he needed someone younger! . . .
I want to go home too. You leave the tip.
Forget your guilt . . . Pfft, taxi! On my lip?
—It's ketchup. Kiss it off. I hailed him first!
Don't touch that handle . . . *You* will get the worst!
You coward—hit and run! Don't cry. Let's walk
Like innocents again across New York.
Let's swagger, arm in waist through Central Park,
And neck defying muggers after dark
And saunter nibbling sauerkraut like grapes.
Let's take our shoes off, shirts off, pants off, traipse
Like infants—parodying our worst and best.
Take off your melancholy, get undressed . . .
I'm serious We'll let our bodies talk
While neighbor elephants and pigeons gawk . . .

The Zoo

I know that you were "acting out"—don't cry.
My wound is healed. That cage is empty—why? . . .
Kids beat the deer? With sticks? This ugly age:
They ought to stick the public in that cage . . .
It isn't hurt. It's terrified of us.
Come here, my love, we too are timorous
Of our civilized aggression, quick
Confused outbursts; no talk, no warning—stick!
You want to cry about this year beat dead?
I didn't change the linen on our bed
For seven months—and you used paper plates
Whenever you ate in? These two are mates.
They can't intuit what hostility
Can suddenly erupt from us in bed
Because your schizophrenic mother fed
You pet food when her schedules broke down,
Because my drunken father tried to drown
My cat with bourbon in the sink, because
I dream of Harpo in a cat's mask, claws
Flaying my father's back, because his wrists
Are really scarred, because two analysts
And seven thousand dollars couldn't stop
Your mother masturbating with a mop
Or mine from comforting her twelve-year-old
Half-lost in nightmare, terrified and cold,
By slipping into bed with him, until
He woke with an erection, broken will.
And yet it's Spring again and we're forgiven.
And if I swear to you that when I'm driven
By guilt and fear to make my tongue a stick,
I'll realize I'm mother's lunatic;
Will you when starved for milk not love please swear
You won't suck off that cow-eyed millionaire?

You see those cherry blossoms bridesmaid white,
Those blue jays half-embracing in flight,
These pigeons shameless in their mating-dance?
We have to give ourselves another chance.
And next year after failure, give another.
Let's have that child. You're stronger than your mother.
Whose hopes, intentions aren't ruined by time?
And chronologically we're in our prime.
In other words Corinna what I'm saying:
We're crazy, wounded, but we are a-maying.

    These animals are growling for their meat.
Robins are pulling earthworms from concrete.
The Delacorte clock's chiming, "It is sunset.
Stop jabbering, divorce is not undone yet."
Come on, let's leave this park, this pubic place
Between the bowed legs of Manhattan, race
That doorman to a cab . . . This driver's mad,
Hold tight! The curbstone's not a launching-pad!
—Or else we're in a farce, that rear-end Death.
He means to shave its paint. Let out your breath.
But close your eyes—he's squirting through two trucks.
They rebound off each other. "Got the fucks!"
Mack Sennett hunches over. "Now a cop!"
We want to walk a little, driver, stop
Right here! We're nearly welded to that bus.
Don't throw that horse laugh at us—Pegasus.

The Jukebox

      This antique store is new. They keep their stuff
Out on the street at night—the owner's tough.
Look at this view of Sheepshead Bay with schooners . . .
Carney and Gleason in *The Honeymooners.*
That campaign button's whose? My eyes are weak.
They're bringing out a jukebox—*that's* antique,
At least as old as me . . . He owns the shop.
Are you attracted to him? . . . No, I'll stop.
Of course enjoy your fantasy! Her ass?
Too flabby for me, but her tits . . . The glass
Is lighting up. What record's wobbling down?
It's Benny Goodman and *Sweet Georgia Brown.*
Look at the crowd that's gathering. I'll bet
This derelict once played the clarinet.
He's tightening the air—his ligature.
His bitter, toothless smile is his armature.
This pimply girl dressed up in Grandma's style
Is awed. "He beats Ted Lewis by a mile!"
I'll bet this Catskill type in hounds tooth pants
Will ask that snazzy meter maid to dance.
You see that woman fussing with her hat?
She's getting set to foxtrot with her cat.
You hear her? "Play a slow one!" There she goes
To Nat King Cole. She's stumbling on her toes:
A ballerina broken by Relief?
The couple waltzing with the handkerchief
Between them are engaged Hasidic Jews.
The crowd ignores the dwarf peddling *The News*
Of murders, bombings, chaos, doomsday, time.
We're innocent, let's dance. The only crime
Is coyness, lady. Let the sun collapse
And night come, we must shoot our craps
Once more, must challenge Death to play.

The jukebox blinks. The song is *Yesterday*.
    A traffic helicopter overhead
Reports that you're refusing to be led
Even in celebration, reports the crowd
Is laughing at us arguing out loud
That you should lead, that I think in clichès
That somehow love remains when love decays,
Reports a man is falling to one knee
And shouting, "Marlene, please re-marry me!"
Reports that you are crying "Yes No Yes,"
Reports that I'm unzippering your dress
And leading you to bed, that you're without
Your diaphragm, "Let's have it now!" I shout,
That you shout back, we're coupling like rhyme,
Reports that we're oblivious to time.
I'm coming—do you hear that baby crying
Across the garden where the wash is drying?

from
Fathering

Hospital

I sit in my father's arm
Chair, David in my lap, lost
In the hospital
—My father is too weak
To ring for help. "What
Time is it?" he asked.
"8 o'clock." "8 o'clock!
I thought it was later!" I
Turn him in his bed and he
Touches my face, his fingers
Already feathers.

Kaddish

Linda sleeps in my mother's
Bed, holding her hand.
David sleeps uncomfortably
In his carriage, and I sleep
In my old bed in the den
Among my father's
Treasures: photos of us,
David at my head . . .
The alarm wakes me. I dress
In my father's clothes and walk
Through a downpour to say Kaddish.

When I return
Schoolchildren fill his lobby.
I pass through them—a shadowy
Man in a gray coat and hat.
The elevator I find
Is empty, except for a
Broken full-length mirror,
A heap of newspapers,
And a box marked "Fragile."
I ascend.

A Message

I click on the telephone
Tape machine, hoping to get
A message from my father.
I let it run back for months.
At the end, only silence.

For David, in the Middle
of the 21ˢᵗ Century

    David, when you are bald
    (Though I hope you're not)
    As you are now
    And rocking in a hammock, remembering
    Something that has no words,
    Pick up this poem
    That has your father in it:
    I've just come home
    From traveling. I
    Shake out my umbrella.
    I lift you from the darkness
    And rock you like a pendulum.
    You tug at my shirt, fascinated
    By the blue and purple rectangles,
    So I take it off.
    You stuff it in your mouth, as you will
    My virtues and my faults. The sun blazes
    And holds us like a photo in the moment
    As you hold this
    As I once held you,
    David.

A Month Later

And it is raining
Still. I lie in bed
Muttering Kaddish
Wrestling myself
Into all angles
Like the Hebrew letters.

Connections

How exquisitely Linda describes her case:
How R.'s mother was cold, his father
Cerebral. I listen, thinking also of space:
Stars collapsing, planets
Breaking from their axes, the careful
Composition of his atoms forever gone.
Linda explains every catastrophe,
How words became his only comfort
Because his father read him to sleep . . .
I think, This door frame is miraculous
And the walls joining it, and the mind's defenses.
And as I drift off and back, and my father
Becomes more of the soil of this planet
Drifting nowhere, David wakes demanding
Linda forget her words and me my reverie
Simply because we love him and he wants to eat.

Foxtrots

I lie in the dark
Listening to foxtrots.
Overhead, my parents
Dance, cheek to cheek.
He dips her. She smiles.
He whirls her from corner to corner.
They are younger than me, masterful
And will never die.
They stop to smoke a cigarette. He
Strikes a match and disappears.
She exits slowly.

Unveiling

My mother stands
In the rain
Too depressed to move,
Staring straight ahead
At the unchiseled
Monument of her own
Grave. I run to her
With an umbrella
Made of my son,
Made of my own childhood
But I can't reach her
While from every
Bewildering
Direction around me,
I hear the thud
Of the rain of earth.

Artificial Light

Heavy rain
Darkening
The wysteria.
I draw the blind
And with a flashlight
Show David
How God
Once amused his soul.
After a while
He scribbles
His reflections
On the ceiling.
On the other hand
My father
Who sold coal
And has no energy
Except, I pray,
His soul's
Lies in the
Dark
Like a fossil.

Walk

After a while I have to get up and walk.
I've had enough of death, enough of it.
Days of my father: nails
Shortened by hammers
Get up and walk
Into a vineyard blue as stigmata
Where there is no reflection but a pond's
Perpetually, aimlessly, wrinkling.

from

Family History

Part I

It's 4 A.M. I've just turned 41.
I'm struggling with my Will all night, my son.
But more than money, I must leave you this
Testament of fact and fiction both,
A Testament, I hope, of family growth.
Read this at my age. This is your genesis.

How can I tell you, where do I begin?
In Poland, a rich old man is asked to choose
Between daughter and mother for his bride.
He sighs, he shrugs, he strokes his whiskered chin.
Shrewdly he takes a season to decide.
There are no pogroms yet to rush the Jews.

So the young one, my great-grandmother, bore five boys:
All loud and strong, fiery like their name,
And one girl, Mary, who told me this tale:
How they worked a farm, fist fought with goys,
Studied nothing but women, stayed out of jail
With bribes, and when the old man died they came

To New York City—Willie, Harry, Joe,
Izzy and Sol. Mary was left behind
And said one day their neighbors refused to show
Her mother *The Forward* that they shared with her.
She went from villager to villager,
From old to young. But not one soul could find

This treasure from America, until
One of the boys' spurned lovers gave her the news:
HARRY FEIRSTEIN SLAIN. No! No! No! No!
WILLI FEIRSTEIN JAILED. From Brody... Jews...

Were brothers ... Harry's stable ... blood ... hook ... Will ...
The letter crumpled in her vertigo.

That very night my great-grandmother sold
Her farm, her livestock, baling hooks and forks
And steered an ocean liner's rail to New York's
Lower East Side. Trying to stay self-controlled
She softly pressed the bell marked "Feirstein."
Then climbed six flights, often pausing to lean

On Mary, then Hallucination: *Gut!*
Her angel Willie at the door? Or Cain?
Mary squeezed my hand when she told me this.
The paper got the melodrama, but
Mixed up the facts. A thug saw Harry kiss
His girl, his doll, his skinny scatterbrain,

And lead her to the shadows of his stable.
They fought. Harry reeled against a table.
The thug leapt on him. Harry reached for his nuts.
The thug reached back and pinned him with a hook
And with another opened up his guts
And made his girlfriend, crazed already, look.

Shrieking she zigzagged down the street. She reached
The barbershop where Willie was stretched out,
Listening to the barber smack his strop
Harry is what? She's talking so damn fast!
Come on, Willie, sit down, sit down, I doubt
Your brother's ... Someone hurry, get a cop!

My Grandpa Willie was over six feet tall.
He swept the thug against the stable wall.
He broke the wrists, the elbows, cheekbones, nose.
He almost drowned him, turning up a hose
Inside the killer mouth before the cops arrived.
Mourning nearly wrecked him. Jail he survived.

Was this a *bubamonsa* Mary told?
The Willie I remember was always old,
Except for brawls I didn't understand:
With anti-semites?—in the Polish bars.
He'd twist their collars with his big right hand
And bang their heads against the walls and cars

And sheepishly come home and down his schnapps
And talk about the ice-plant that he lost
In cards to Schwartz who made "a mint" on it.
It took till now to fully know its cost:
My father's business failures and my flops
And why my father treated me like shit

When I became an adolescent, and
Why I dressed like a motorcycle knight
And (worse for me) refused to understand
His need for money and security
—Till 41, when I would try to write
A poem in praise of domesticity!

*

On my mother's side were Sam and Annie,
Mild second-cousins from the Russian Pale,
Seemingly just my Jewish Gramps and Granny
Until, of course, I heard my uncle's tale.
I loved my Grandma like the birds she fed.
She spoke just a few English words, like "Fred."

Sam was a tailor, barely five feet tall,
The only one in his Society
Who could write English, and so became the scribe
Of what now seems a medieval tribe.
Unlike Willie, who laughed at piety,
Sam lived for *shul*—a former Legion Hall

In the South Bronx, then a Jewish ghetto.
Their street's no longer there, burnt down, Baretto.
But New York then? I sigh a Jewish sigh:
My mother never had to lock our door.
She was friends with every neighbor on the floor
—Although that 1950's clear blue sky

Was full of fallout from the A-bomb tests
As Sam often (so goes my uncle's tale) burst
Into rages, fucked other women, cursed
Annie in from of their children, in front of guests.
It took me forty years to understand
Why my mother had to have the upper hand

And never talked of family history.
No one did but Mary. The rest I know
I pumped from second cousins, uncles, aunts
Who never dreamt it something to bestow.
And *Yiddishkeit*? A shameful mystery.
This wasn't only true of immigrants:

Americans obliterate the past,
Not understanding that to "Make It New"
Really means rediscovering tradition.
My father would have laughed at this admission,
"Some rebel!" I was an iconoclast
By asking questions like a greenhorn Jew!

—Especially about the Schechter's main
Historical disaster: The Pogrom,
More dreadful to my mother than The Bomb
To me because it happened in her village.
Warned, they hid inside a burned-out train,
Hearing the killing, rape, and pillage

—Three Jewish girls of twelve and ten and five,
Their mother an hysteric "with a heart

So bad," they didn't think she'd stay alive
Long enough to shepherd them to Sam
In the South Bronx. Didn't he give a damn,
Not sending for them after seven years?

The mails were halted (as the tale was told)
By the Russian Revolution. After, Sam
Sent them his meager savings and, with gold
They earned running a Bolshevik tea shop,
They bribed their way through borders, didn't stop
Until they reached a boat in Rotterdam

And, on the voyage here, an orange crate
Fell, opening a gash in my mother's head
—Delirium! Worse than the pain, the dread
That on Ellis Island she'd be turned around.
Not understanding her, I blew up when I found
Her waiting for me when I came home late

—Deliberately at 3 or 4 or dawn,
Drinking like Willie but with a gentile friend.
And when she nagged and when I got withdrawn
And when she nagged some more and when I cursed
Her out like Sam, I couldn't comprehend
That by my maleness I had done my worst.

My mother grew up in a tenement:
Two tiny rooms, the toilet in the hall
—But no pogroms. Just little heat, high rent.
She was 12 in the first grade, sat in the back,
Spoke only Yiddish, her teacher was black.
But thanks to Sam and Annie she was small

And smart, and monthly skipped a grade. But when
She turned 15, she had to give up school.
Though Sam was an outstanding man in *shul*,
He was a tailor in a cleaning store.

As a poet has his craft and nothing more,
He did free-lance piece work, needle for his pen.

So my mother had to learn to type and file
And sacrifice her happiness for others.
In gratitude, her parents gave her brothers.
My mother took her fortune with a smile,
A warming smile—Nettie was a beauty
Who tried to teach her teen-aged rebel duty

And what she called "the value of a dollar."
But I refused or couldn't understand
That phrase or learn to love work for work's sake
Or that she couldn't easily give or take
Anything to me, from me—though I'd holler
Like Sam and wind up infantile, unmanned.

For thirteen years she struggled for each dime.
Deprived of childhood, her mother's mother,
She typed all day, then bathed or fed a brother.
Never enough money, never enough time.
I learned how much she gave up when she died,
Depleted like a pauper, nullified.

*

My father, Artie, though, had money.
Willie owned a horse cart with an ice-machine.
I still remember one Spring morning—sunny,
Smelling of horse manure and flowers.
I rode it through Manhattan's streets for hours
Spitting the pits out of a tangerine,

A real Middle European journey,
Romanians, Czechs, Poles, all bought his ice.
The Lower East Side then was Paradise.

My father was the eldest of five *kinder*
—Annabelle, Sylvia, Renee, and Bernie.
Unlike my mother, nothing would hinder

Artie but family *mishigas:*
                              My pretty,
Grandma Fanny, jilted by her lover,
A German Jew who thought himself above her,
Married Willie as an act of spite.
She was a cultured lady from a city,
But Willie never even learned to write,

Signing what checks she'd let him with a scrawl
Each day she'd taunt him. *"Buvan,"* she would scream.
"You're good for nothing but to drink and brawl."
How could my father define himself like him
Or, as he tried to, be his antonym
And still not suffer awful self-esteem?

He put his eyes out at our kitchen table
When Willie, now the thug in Harry's stable
Cut him, cut Oedipus to the quick.
I tried to rescue him, said "This is sick,"
Under my breath. But being Oedipus
Myself and scared, I didn't make a fuss.

But at that kitchen table in my teens,
My rage blew all my shame to smithereens.
When Artie laughed and called me "sensitive"
I couldn't make excuses for his hate,
I couldn't keep my eyes down on my plate.
When you're a man, my son, I'll let you live!

Four months before my birth, Grandma Fanny died.
Although the doctors told her I might smother,
My mother hemorrhaging with me went to her side,

Climbing down flights, up flights—a heroine—
And promised she would take the family in:
Grandpa, three sisters, and a younger brother.

I wouldn't write this passage with such malice
If Nettie didn't tell me this with pride,
Oblivious to what I might have felt.
So by my Grandma's side my mother knelt,
A Princess ready to possess the palace.
God blessed her and spared her infanticide.

*

I'll try to reconstruct those early years,
Before my sister's birth, when my mother hoped
I'd be for her what Cossack Russia killed:
A little girl, a Momma to her fears.
Somehow I think I knew it and I coped
And tried to please her. Feisty though I was, strong-willed,

I waited till my teens to be a male
Openly. How I needed Artie's strength
To free me from her when she dressed me up
At three in pink, my hair a girlish length.
But Artie seemed to have his father's *kup*
And played the ogre in her fairy tale,

Threatening to cut my hands off when I'd strum
My penis as I would my violin.
He'd seen my jealous sibling who'd assist her,
A mute when my fat aunt, my mother's sister,
Called me his girl—so sensitive, so thin."
—But stopped when they discovered lithium.

I couldn't always hide that I was strong,
And defied my mother when her back was turned.

I beat up other children till I learned
Nice Jewish boys don't do such things—although
I saw my father lay three neighbors low,
They'd lecture me that "fisticuffs were wrong."

They did the same with sex. Ignoring my cock
They keep me in their room till I was six,
And when they fist fought kissing (so I thought)
And woke me screaming, they would mock
Me for imagining their noisy kicks,
Tell me that I was dreaming, overwrought.

Our childhoods die in many subtle ways,
Not simply from abuse, not simply from neglect.
As startled butterflies are trapped and pinned,
We're snared by those whom we would least suspect,
Then fixed in rigid attitudes—in praise
Of what could not be loved but disciplined.

My sister couldn't go to sleep at night
Without her bed sheets almost sewed in tight
As if that could protect her from her dreams.
I did the opposite. I fled in slow motion,
Sleepwalking across the desert, ocean,
Avenged myself on them with hellish screams

Until my mother would up in my bed.
I'd dream that we cut off my father's head
And, Nazis, used it for a bowl of flowers.
We'd lie like that, mother and child, for hours.
And then I'd leave her to the wrath of God
Who counted for a Cossack firing squad.

And so I grew, twisted but disinclined
To play the ghetto Jew my mother's way:
The female male, the scapegoat girls, the gay

Rebel. Or on the other hand, the grind
In school, afraid to battle gentile boys,
Like Nettie in the shtetl stoned by goys.

Whom am I kidding? None of us escape
Completely childhood guilt or childhood rape.
The poet in me is my female self,
The Muse my mother whom I want to please,
Seducing me to write for her, the tease,
Proud of the books I lay upon my shelf.

*

Caution! Danger! I can easily condemn
Myself alone for causing family friction,
Condemn my adolescent rage like them
And make my childhood seem a happy fiction
—Although that New York shtetl had such pleasure,
The kind we see in books like *Jewish Treasures*.

I came from an extended family:
My grandfather, parents, sister, uncle, aunts
—Nine people living in five rooms, and more
Visiting weekends, bulging through the door:
A chuckling fat man crammed in too tight pants.
How *could* my parents have their privacy?

They could have put me in the living room, that's how!
That's why I can't be really schmaltzy now
About that place, and yet, and yet... Caution,
Danger, I can make the same contortion
Psychologically now as I did then.
And as they pulled my penis, dull my pen.

The building that we lived in was a town
Taking up half the block and looking down

Miles of nineteenth-century tenements
Where fathers drank, and foul arguments
Exploded daily into child abuse,
Where women cringed, prayed for a state of truce

And nurtured flowers on their fire-escapes
And tried to keep the coal dust out with drapes
And plastic covers on each couch and chair,
And brushed their pre-delinquent children's hair
And Sunday mornings shined their Sunday shoes
For church—where they were taught to hate the Jews,

Where my best friends were taught, when I was seven,
That I killed Christ, I'd never go to Heaven.
"Mommy," I cried, "How could I cause the Fall?
Besides, what's wrong with that? I like that season."
"Don't let them bother you." "But what's the reason?"
She took me by the hand and brought a shawl

And lit the Sabbath candles. "Don't forget
No one will love you but your family, Fred,
And take you in no matter what you do.
The best of them will call you 'Dirty Jew'
When they're upset. Don't be misled."
David, why do I tell you this vignette?

There was such comfort in that family
Despite its craziness when I was small,
Chattering to my mother while she dressed
(In latency I never felt distressed)
About my schoolwork and my basketball . . .

My Uncle Bernie was an army scout,
The only white with an Apache troop
Holding their breaths for signs of Japanese,

Each moving branch a sword of Damocles.
When I was three, the army let him out.
He'd claim he was a medic there, but whoop

Sadly when I'd blast him with my gun.
He was a boxer, wanted to turn pro,
Fight Willie Pep before the War broke out.
But Willie wouldn't let his handsome son
Who looked like Garfield's double do it, so
Malaria was Bernie's final bout.

He would up in the post office at night
And selling coal and oil accounts by day
And on the weekends taught me basketball
And how to comb my pompadour and say,
"Come here, baby," and how to fight despite
Great suffering. I learned that from them all,

Especially my father's baby sister
Renee, whose mother died when she was eight.
They didn't tell her, packed her off to camp
And kept the lie up when she said she missed her.
Frost-bitten, Renee learned to amputate
All memory of her mother and to stamp

Out all her feelings of abandonment
And be a strong and independent child
Who never acted anything but mild
And never called my parents negligent
And called me, not her nephew, but her brother.
She told me if she hadn't me to mother,

To teach to read, to Cha Cha, Lindy, sing,
She would have died of constant soldiering.
Her destiny, relentlessly ironic,
Dealt her, when she reached her mother's age, chronic

Leukemia. The spleen she couldn't vent
Again depriving her of nourishment.

*

I can remember everything since one,
Poets having egos that do not repress.
But it's painful to recall Aunt Annabelle,
Except for small things: the pretty way she'd dress,
Her desperate need to go out and have fun
And smoke and use words like "the creep" and "swell."

Willie called this fifteen year old "a whore"
For merely kissing someone at the door
Or coming in a half an hour late
Or "lazy" when she didn't scrub a plate
Or serve him tea when he demanded it.
She'd keep her eyes down fearing he would hit,

And seemed mysterious and soft to me.
I used to want to give her all my toys.
She'd laugh and kiss my forehead tenderly
And tell her friends she only wanted boys
Like me when she got married. What a hell
Her life became, this dove, this Annabelle.

At eighteen she left home to marry Lee,
A wheeler-dealer, skinny as a whip,
Who when a business deal collapsed would smack
Her silly or would verbally attack.
I'd watch her cringe when he'd warn, "Shut your lip"
—Or shake her head, her eyes wide, panicky.

I'm drinking milk at her white kitchen table.
She's trying desperately to smile at me.
I tell her that I hate this "creep," this Lee.

She tells me he means well but he's unstable,
Then she falls silent with a frightening stare,
Mindlessly turning hands of solitaire.

At last she died of cancer at my age,
Of schizophrenia and drugs and shock.
She called home every night in grief or rage
And Grandma talked to her around the clock.
Her house was dark and run down, full of deal
Dressers and chairs embroidered with chenille.

*

At five I thought Aunt Sylvia romantic
In fox fur, nylons, spiked heels, pillbox hat
—A working girl beneath a John Sloan El.
The others didn't think of her like that
But as a spinster, unlike Annabelle.
Though she was 27, she was frantic

And said despite my protests she was "plain"
And sat her rimless glasses on my nose:
"Boys don't make passes at girls who wear glasses
Or feminists who wear designer clothes."
She'd prink a mocking smile and bat her lashes
And say she should have been a scatterbrain

And I'd protest and tell her she was funny.
She'd laugh, "You'll have to play John Wayne
One day with fists, one day with money,"
And crack her gum like Ginger Rodgers tapped.
I'd dance to it, my baseball bat my cane.
At every little thing I did, she clapped.

She left me for a chubby soldier, Al,
Who didn't dance, who couldn't tell a joke.

They'd sit too quiet on her Hope Chest, smoke
Chesterfields, plan her move out of the house.
"Please take me with you, aren't you my gal?"
I'd wedge between them, tugging on her blouse.

They bought me off with bubblegum and married
And ran a boarding house on the West Side.
Al proved laconic, lazy. She grew harried.
Later Aunt Mary toldme that their life
Mimicked Willie's bickering with his wife.
Her jokes turned dull, her spirit petrified.

At times a family history is Soap.
Dear Mary had retarded children, all
The others died, like Sylvia, of cancer.
Misfortune asks a questions, finds no answer.
Thank God we have genetics, not the Fall.
And so with research (modern prayer) there's hope

And hope with psychotherapy when done
With understanding of how we, though smart,
Will fall into our mother's, father's part
With wife or mother, daughter, husband, son.
Like her two sisters, my mock-scatterbrain
Internalized and strangled from the pain

That killed her father Willie stroke by stroke.
I knew a different Zeydie Willie who
Hitched horses to his bedposts with silk ties
Painted with cowpokes under Western skies,
Who taught me bronco busting and lassoing
And way past bedtime sneaked me to a zoo

Of handmade shadows on our moonlit wall.
He taught me every barnyard mating call.
He smuggled me beneath his massive coat

To every Preston Sturges film for free.
"Follow the bouncing ball"—it's in my throat.
I loved him. He unequivocally loved me.

*

And as I write this, you are sound asleep
It's 4 A.M. and barely 4 degrees.
I'm Willie in my hounds tooth ice man's cap.
I write a little, take a little nap
And wake to cover you so you won't freeze
When the stream stops, and count so I won't weep

For Artie dead on January 4
At 4 A.M. when you were 4 months old
—Numbers are crisp and comprehensible—
For Nettie stranded, seriously ill
With irreversible depression. "Hold
Me," she would tug me like a child, "Hold more!"

But when it lifted, manically snapped
That I did nothing for her. Yet I knew
From watching her fight hard to play with you,
She loved me as she could, and I loved her.
I do not want to be her slanderer
Because she made me feel abandoned, trapped,

And yet when I remember how she made
Me see my past in you by threatening
To leave you if you didn't kiss her cheek . . .
Terrified, you surrendered and she stayed
—Not for long. Her ego and her heart were weak.
No love, no medicine, no talk could bring

Her back, when Artie like her father left.
She finally became my child, bereft
Of every pretense. Everything she tried,

She tried for you. I found her when she died,
Stretched out across her bead—a heart attack.
Her tongue, stuck out (at me I thought), was black.

*

When I was twelve, my world collapsed like this.
Bernie and Renee left and Willie died
Within six months. I'd sit in darkness, stupefied
Till Nettie came in asking for a kiss
And tried to cuddle me like I was four
Or, worse, she'd call me from her bedroom door

And pick a fight while she was dressing,
Rolling her stocking slowly up, perfuming
Around her bra with, naturally, *Tabu*
She was the Russian, I the speechless Jew.
She'd wonder, smiling, why I stood there fuming.
And while I stammered, rapidly regressing,

She'd have me clasp her necklace, zip her dress.
My rather watched her (fully clothed) provoke me
And noticed nothing but my building rage.
He'd make a fist, threatening to choke me.
She'd say "*Luz oyn zaree*, it's just a stage,"
And tell me, "Business gives him enough stress,

He doesn't need to take this crap from you!"
I'd tell him she was instigating us
And that our brawls were titillating her.
At last we came to blows. "You panderer,"
I screamed. "You know, this is incestuous!"
And walked out shouting at them both to "screw,"

And threw away my books and greased my hair,
Dressed in a white scarf, brown leather jacket
And told my puzzled friends to call me "Ace."

Though it would make me clogged up and grimace
I filled my room with smoke, and with a blar-
Ing music that my father called "a racket."

Contemptuous I bought a tenor sax
My father rightly called by "battle-ax."
And so the Feirsteins in three short years
Moved from the shtetl into rock and roll
And danced the '50's dance they called "The Stroll."
It simply took some nylons and brassieres.

*

But every action that we take exists
In multiplicities of time. And so
I also was a hurt twelve year old
Who, when his sister messed up in school, was told
To keep his urgent needs *pianissimo*.
They sniped at me, I felt, like terrorists:

For having skinny legs when I ran track,
For being much too short for basketball,
For getting 90—"Why not 95?"—
In English. What I heard was, *Do not thrive.*
How dare you walk when Rosalee can't crawl?
Guilty, I'd stay a mute when they'd attack.

And I was also three, trying to please
My father, me—*who's Nettie's little girl?*
Look I'm a hood with sideburns and a curl!
Anyone touches me, I'll break their knees,
Like Zeydie Willie in his brother's stable.
I'm Cain to my internal Abel.

Except, I've learned whenever we rebel,
We act out what our parents had to quell
In them when they were young, and really miss

That reckless self they lost through cowardice,
As Artie, though he'd shake his balding head,
Was in his day a hood like "Crazy Fred."

Artie the businessman who hardly spoke
Would often tell this story like a joke:
Of how we went to college for a year
But didn't study, guzzled gentile beer
And played around with (wink, wink) Southern Belles
And one day driving with a bunch of swells,

Boasted he'd sell his Packard for a shave,
Haircut and manicure. "Give him the works,"
They said, "He's not some kike, he's suave."
Nettie to my astonishment laughed too,
Nettie the frugal, persecuted Jew
Who called my rowdy friends a bunch of jerks.

And so I learned to scorn my macho pose,
Rebelled against it, once again—at him.
Or so I thought and quietly wrote poems
And—"Freddy, are you sick?"—spoke only Ohms.
"Nettie, is he a beatnik now?" "God knows,
He certainly looks *shva* enough and grim."

"So be a Village Bum, a Village Helion.
I think you're spitting in our face with Verse!"
No, actually what started as rebellion
Would turn me into Nettie's little girl,
A girl without a penny in her purse.
I'd learn I had it easy with the *Merle*.

from
City Life

The Shawl

1. Siddhartha Dove

We screw, then you lecture me on "The East"
Because you say my better half is black,
Then mock that white gal's photo on my desk:
That was my wife. That was no playful smack
Across your ass. Don't say, "Listen at least!"

My daughter also had contempt for whites.
She called herself "Historically deprived."
She missed out on The War and Civil Rights.
She developed that same missionary smile
Toward me—"decadent for having thrived

In a Western meditative racket." Her eyes
Crossed when I said, "Do ghetto social work,"
As a 1940's starlet might've looked
At the proposal of a soda jerk.
My training taught me never to advise

Anyone. Mulattoes never know their place.
This was her room, usually a mess.
She tried to sketch her idols: Chairman Mao,
Like you loved "poor Che"—and Herman Hesse.
Some politics! That's her baby-face

The say she turned into Siddhartha Dove.
Her Deide doll, her bike, her leather thongs,
Her button from the rally for Reverend Moon.
That hair's her relic . . . "What radical's?" King Kong's!
Her great-great grandmother's face: an octoroon

Runaway—a genuine Matthew Brady.
She married and became an English lady
And moved to India. Resemblance strange?
Her water pipe... My wife was dead, I did my best!
That pain, not Hesse, sent her on her "quest."

She painted my army knapsack baby-pink.
She painted her t-shirt with her guru's face.
She painted a red dot on her forehead.
"This country doesn't give me growing space,"
She said. "A shrink's daughter doesn't shrink

From exploration." Her No Smoking sign.
I bought it, angry at her innocence:
"You will not find pollution in Bombay."
She sent me this sealed vial for evidence,
To sniff the air around her guru's shrine.

After a while: months between her notes—
"Afghanistanis shower me with dope...
I had a child, I sold him, that's okay...
Don't worry, I won't try the snake and rope:
I got a gig this summer herding goats."

She died in bed, a Delhi gutter, cut
More often than a Christian saint.
Her begging cup ran over with her blood.
A Third World proselytizer shouldn't faint!
A begging gang had sewn her mild mouth shut,

A lesson for the other Hesse kids.
Never again would she eat their precious trash.
Never again compete for *Baksheesh* (alms).
In scorn they blacked her dying face with ash.
None had the Western grace to close her lids...

No, stay. I want your company tonight.
I hate your politics, but I love your sex . . .
You'll need to joke when you're my age . . . I'll make
You give up Arabs? Keep you arabesques
And move a little closer to the right.

2. The Eyes

A colored psychoanalyst?
Sorry. You want me to sit here?
You look half-Jewish. My wife's friend
Belle *nudged* me to come. I hope
You're not a Muslim. Do you have
A son? Sorry. "Why?"
I can see pain in your eyes
—My field is ophthalmology,
Or was. I'm not retired, but
I can't work. I guess that's why I've come . . .

I joined a *shul* to give my son a home
After I died—with nostalgic smells:
Satin and parchment. Who believed
The Auschwitz God could hear a prayer?
Him!: "When the black plague destroyed
Half Europe's Christians, they fell to their knees
And found cause in their own lack
Of faith." I wanted to stop there
—The satin, the parchment. My wife
Ignored me, dug out her mother's shawl
And *bentsht lichtn* each Friday night.
And we had seders every spring,
And sang in grass Quonset huts
On Sukkos, and wept Kol Nidre nights . . .

You want to hear "a dream?" My son
Drifts from heaven in a parachute

Dawning, a baby in a swing,
At eighteen pretty as his mother,
Eyes the color of Israel's flag.
SUNSET IN LEBANON—A Dream
With Titles Or, A Dream With Guns!
I mock analysis as I do
All faiths because, because my son . . .
They brought him back from *Yisroel*
With heaven where his eyes were!

Back to "the problem," why I've come:
At 6 A.M. I leave for *shul*
With my bad heart, trudging
Through drifts of snow.
I, not my son, say Kaddish.
I sit with my forehead
Pressed on the bench in front of me
Till *Maariv* when I snap
To attention and mumble more . . .
You seem to know what *Maariv* is
—All these Yiddishisms.
There's something in your eyes. Are you
A *Falasha*? Something kindred . . .

So I sit like a Talmudist
In *shul* all day
Eating a sandwich from a paper bag
Or curled up, snoring, till the sun sets
—And then it's up like a believer
Waiting for Kaddish in the evening prayers . . .
But if I don't endure these rituals,
How will he find me
When I come to Heaven,
A blur, a shadow
Blabbering because his wife—and Belle—
Are worried for his heart,

A wife who bentshes lichtn still,
His picture like a saint's
In front of her except, except he's draped
In that same shawl—that flag
In which we buried him!

Excuse me, but your eyes seem blurred.
Has my story moved you,
Or have you heartache from a son?
You won't say . . . Silence . . . Where am I going?
I can get the same from Kaddish?
That picture on your desk, is she
Your daughter, draped in a sari,
Red dot on her forehead, eyes fogged
With that same religious look?
A nod. I need a friend to share
My tragedy, and you have your technique.
I'm sorry. When you see Belle,
Please tell her not to worry. She's blessed
With a pregnant daughter and a selfish son.

YIDDISHISMS, etc.

    nudged-pestered

    shul-synagogue

    bensht lichtn-blessed (the Sabbath) candles

    seders-Passover meals

    Sukkos-Harvest Festival

    Kol Nidre-prayer of atonement

    davning-praying

    Yisroel-Israel

    Kaddish-prayer for the dead

    Maariv-the evening service

    Falasha-Ethiopian Jew

3. Belle's Café

The census-taker? Show me proof. Come in.
Excuse my bathrobe. Sit. Didn't I mail
My form to you? I thought I filled it in.
I don't have much to offer, just a cup
Of tea, maybe a piece of mandlebread.
They used to call my kitchen "Belle's Café"
And fed me with their troubles while they ate ...
It's nicer, yes? to sit and work this way.
You write. The medication makes me shake.
See how this tea cup rattles? Don't write *that*!
"Stone" was my maiden name. My husband's dead.
Over a year ago. In May. I've got
One daughter and a grandson and a son.
Excuse me but sometimes it helps to pace.
No, don't come back tomorrow. I can talk.
In fact, if it's a good day, I might take
A walk to the market with my friend. She
Has troubles! Yet *she* is a citizen.
Her husband is incapable of work.
An atheist, he sits in *shul* all day
And I can't sit for thirty seconds straight!
My therapist, who tries with me, will spout,
"We move between the poles of love and hate,
Trying to merge, trying to separate."
So, where's my household?—Question 5—The grave!
I'm sorry. You're a stranger and, in spite
Of all the help I get, I can't
Be brave. Not like my friend who lost her son.
I'm not a person but a part of one.

When my husband died, I didn't cry, not once
And we did everything together, talked
On the phone a dozen times a day, slept
Together, shopped together, and when he drove
I spouted the directions. Now I've none.

And so put down for Question 6: a half
A person lives at 20-55,
Dressed in a bathrobe, boring a stranger,
Pacing to show that half is still alive!
I'm sorry for these outbursts. You've just come
To take the facts. You're probably not the type
Who even wants to know what made a life
Statistical. That's why you've chosen this work.
But for the future, take my case to heart:
Those who live too close or far apart
From others are the same. One can't survive
Alone. The other seriously doubts
That he's alive. I'm like your mother, right?
And you're like mine—and also like my son
Who works as an accountant, and who calls
Me, even in this state, "The Know-It-All,"
And visits, if I'm lucky, once a month,
And lets me tell my troubles to his wife
By phone! And now it's time for you to go
And time for me to rest before I pace
—Between love for my husband and hate,
Trying to merge, trying to separate.

4. The Grandson

> "Me reweth, Marye, thy sone and thee"
> ("SUNSET IN CALVARY")

I'm not a pretty woman, never was.
My nose is surgically small, my eyes slitty.
My hair, even when combed, looks electrified.
My legs, poor things, are like a pelican's.
But men have always liked my being witty,
Especially my soldier—he was young,
Talkative, generous, blond, blue-eyed
—His eyes were cowish, a shade of dung!

I overstepped myself again—no tact.
This room is sheltered, quiet, don't you think?
A bed that cranks up like an ak-ak gun,
A vase of exploding roses.
 Shutup shutup shutup shutup
Are you a male nurse, social worker, shrink?
—Angelic in white, a beard like Moses.
A pelican's some symbol for a Jew.
And the good doctors of Jerusalem
Cut the cord from his neck, turning him pink.
What's that gurgling, bubbling in the sink?
Nothing. Petals folding like two hands in prayer.
My soldier was 19. I am 31.
Homesick New Yorkers making *Aliyah*.
We made love one night, one night, that's all.
Enough to start the deadly birth: the Fall
Of Isaac was his name—appropriate?
Ten pounds of scrunchy fat and smiles,
And talkative? He wouldn't shutup.
Some nights I told him I'd mute him—he'd smile.
Some nights I told him I'd give him away,
He was driving me crazy—no sleep—he'd smile.
Baby, I'd say, I've got a delicate *kup*
With fantasies, shmantasies driving me wild.
I'd sing to him, Go to sleep, drop dead, my child.
Cut to a kibbutz, rest cure, no street
Noises, no cars, cabs, buses, trucks.
Smash a champagne bottle against the sky—
Stars! Carve a piece of feta cheese—moon!
And blessèd exhaustion after a mute day's work.
And how I loved to see him in the mornings
Kick at his mobile, blue-eyed. Were his father's dung?
Oh he was handsome, what's-his-name, and young.
Alarms, alarms, snatch babies out of their cribs,
Running across courtyard, down to the shelter
 Shutup shutup shutup shutup:
The terrorists are really coming,

Triggers of Kalashnikovs they're strumming,
And I am rocking him to sleep and humming.
But shutup shutup *Sha! They'll kill us all,
Unless you quiet him!* I take my shawl
And wrap it like a shroud around his face.
His eyes are frantic—shh—a second more.
I hear them, don't you, running past the door?
Why doesn't he answer me—Yitzhak?
Isaac? Shmendrik? Aren't I witty?
They never told me I'd be pretty.
But I've become a tragic heroine.
I'm praised and mourned in all of the cafés.
Are you an angel glowing there in white,
Or am I doped by all these pills I've taken?
Green ones, yellow ones, purple ones, pink.
I know I should get up and vomit in the sink
Or stand inside a shower leaking gas.
I'll lie beside my baby, and the grass
Will cover us brown as dung, and when the birds
Try to waken us for the Apocalypse,
We'll whisper to them, both in baby-talk,
Shutup shutup shutup shutup.

from "The Psychiatrist At The Cocktail Party: A Verse Play"

Larry Corners the Psychiatrist

Look who's standing in my bedroom door!
Give me your coat, Ben. Glad you could come
To one of my fund-raising bashes.
This one is for that man from Quistador.
Startling, these guys in khaki and mustaches.
Try an hors d'oeuvre. The catering is yum.

Where's Mary? . . . Jeez, does she have a fever?
I hope it's just the flu and nothing more.
Even you'd be a hypochondriac
With my mother—it was so hard to leave her.
I wish Mary wasn't flat on her back
I wanted her to see my new décor.

It's Pop-Colonial, a parody:
Brighton bamboo, but painted Third World red.
The knicknacks are from 42nd Street,
Las Vegas, and Disneyland: *our* ivory
But crafted out of plastic—Go on, eat—
And not one single elephant shot dead.

Mary would have loved our rebel guest,
An illustration of her Ph. D.
On Latin intellectuals cum killer.
I think this baby far outstrips the rest.
He has a Harvard social work degree
And still reads shrink books. God, I think he'd thrill her.

The women love him, so he said to Joyce
Jokingly. Doc, while I still have your ear,
I want to tell you something. Please don't smirk.
I think I may be making the wrong choice
In getting married. (Hi, Steve.) Come stand here.
Each time I get engaged, my goddamn quirk

Obsesses me—is that the proper word?
Some aspect of her body starts to look
—Her breasts, her neck, even the way she walks—
Like Mom's or Sis's. Isn't that absurd?
I've haunted bookstores, looking for a book
About this. You know my shrink never talks

But simply nods or says, "In time we'll see."
Except that lately I can't get it up!
When Joyce lies on her side, her torso's curve
Is Mom's! I know what you must think of me:
    Our little Larry got a crazy kup.
    Our little Shmedipus ain't got the nerve,

I hear my coffee magnate father say,
    That's why I left a trust fund for the jerk.
    He can't support himself in love or work.
That's not the truth. You want to hear it, Ben?
You want to hear the only, maddening way
A woman makes my soldier stiffen?

Remember when I first came on to Joyce
—Before her husband died, when she was his?
Exactly when I first came on to Liz,
Nancy, and Beth. All mothers of a boy
Rebellious as I was! I should keep my voice
Down. Can you hear me? I hope this won't destroy

Our friendship, Ben. Don't smile. I'm serious.
Joyce was your student, sort of like your child.

You see Renee dancing? It drives me wild
To watch her luring husband. It
Makes me absolutely delirious.
I think deep down I can't leave Momma's tit.

I'm boring you, you hear this every day
And write that sex is often infantile.
I will not toddle down the wedding aisle,
Hoping that once your Joyce becomes my wife
This craziness will somehow go away,
And that at forty-two I'll change my life!

Please think about this as you mingle here.
Joyce shouldn't have to tough this out with me,
Her husband dead. I bet her son is gay.
I wonder of I have a buried fear
Of "hamasexuality," as Dad would say.
I can't believe that I am fidgety

Around Renee, and that the Meat King
Her husband—that fat, that ignorant, that crass
Wholesale butcher is what I really crave,
That somewhere in me I am conjuring
His slipping a long bratwurst up my ass.
I am my mother's not my father's slave!

I was attracted to Renee in school,
Before the Meat King crawled into her bed.
But then I wasn't rich enough, an heir;
Just a Momma's boy, a cheerleader, a fool.
But now, however, I am debonair,
A boy to flirt with, not that my father's dead.

To Larry Who Doubts He Should Marry

Larry, imagine after dying that your soul
Wakes up in a barren, rural home
In Quistador—genetically a gnome,
But smart, aware of living in a hole

From watching t.v., watching men like you
Throw parties where they somberly confess
They feel powerless when they undress,
Or get excited by some rebel's coup.

Imagine *being* like you're feeling, Larry,
And think concretely of your peasants' lives,
The helplessness they suffer with their wives,
And how they'd laugh to hear you might not marry

Because you're too "obsessed" to make a home
With Joyce who gives you what you'd rather give
Politically—to strangers. Larry, live
As if you're not inhabiting a gnome.

All day I hear my patients curse their fate,
How psychologically they re-create
Their parents tyrannizing them with guilt
Until their penises refuse to tilt,
How history seems passed down in their genes:
Oedipus zipping down his gabardines

And, like you, finding Guess who? Mother!
Abel getting all A's, despite his brother
Who beats him nightly when the lights are out,
And wakes up in adulthood wracked by doubt.
I don't speak glibly when I say rejoice,
Suffer your neurosis. But marry Joyce.

Larry's Mother

You're Doctor Struthers, aren't you?
The former mentor of his fiancée
I'm Larry's mother. Call me Bea.
Larry never thinks of introducing me,
As if he's lying and I might give him away,
Or set up an intriguing rendezvous.

Though Larry's Harvard, I am crass
And all his friends find me refreshing. So,
What do you think? You like the merchandise?
You're puzzled, but you giggled twice.
Am I a psychiatric type that you don't know,
Or just an agèd piece of ass?

I was a Catskill comedienne.
True. Always "on," always playing a part
Till Larry's father, may he rest in peace,
Insisted on calling me, not Bea, but Beatrice,
And that I had more than a mouthpiece—a heart.
That isn't cockamamie, Ben.

If I might be presumptuous
(Who me?), I'd like to solicit
(Please no blushing, no erection)
Your thoughts about this insurrection
Larry's supporting now in Quistador. No thoughts on it?
Try the stuffed shrimp: they're scrumptious.

Tell me if this is self-destructive: Quistador
Borders the country where we import
Our coffee beans. Larry says
To me, only to me, Juarez
Will leave our crops alone if we support
His cause, if we serve schnapps to the señor.

But now, of course, I overhear my Larry
Talk only of ideals to everyone.
Did he reveal this other side to you?
He's not your patient, there is no taboo
Involved. Believe me, it ain't fun
To ask you. Your pet Joyce he plans to marry

Don't know, or else won't say. That shrimp is good.
The caterer was my lover. So,
Knowing Larry, what do you think?
What will you have to drink?
Take your time, but tell me what you know.
Our coffee business now is thriving, knock on wood.

But if it goes, and I am gone,
What happens to my son? How will he fend
For himself—he's never done it—on his wits?
Under pressure Larry quits.
You know how as a kid he used to defend
Himself in school? He'd befriend the scum,

Or give them money so they wouldn't beat him up.
Like now—I never thought of it!
You see what happens even talking to a shrink?
Your golden silence made me think!
He's buying protection, the little shit.
Let me pour *our* coffee in your cup.

Joyce

Hello, Doctor . . . Why am I looking glum?
I didn't realize, Ben. Show me the look.
I'm glad that you could leave your work and come . . .
See patients on a Saturday? Silly,
I thought you might be working on your book!
Where's Mary? I hope she isn't ill. She

Doesn't take much care of your . . . her body. Larry
Is somewhere back there asking someone if
He finally ought to take the plunge and marry.
What do I want to do? Pour me a stiff
Drink and I'll tell you. Sometimes, Mine Herr Shrink
—Always—I want to run away in time
And be your fawning student, whoops! I think
There's more than scotch and soda in this. I'm
Getting high on talking to you. I hate
Larry's parties for these dwarfs of history
Like that one with the beard, that second-rate
Castro with his obligatory bad-
Mouthing America. Here's my son.

* * *

You know Dr. Struthers. How's the party, Steve?
I'm glad you like the Guest of Honor. He
(Larry claims) will soon take over Quistador
And bring equality to everyone.
Larry is raising money for his war.
Yes, try your Spanish out on him. I'm glad
You're interested. But tell me when you leave.

* * *

What is he doing? Just driving me mad.
But I don't want to talk about Steve yet.
The music's playing, and I want to dance.
I want to close my eyes and fantasize
That I'm in college with the power to
(Don't laugh) destroy your analytic stance.
That's what I thought when I looked up at you
This way, knowing of course you liked the look.
I know because you'd either rub your eyes
Or look for something (safety?) in your book,

Or ask me questions like you're doing now.
I haven't laughed all week. *Stop, Joyce. Ask him how
His patients are.* How's Mary? Glad she's healthy,
And Larry's well, and Larry's very wealthy.

Renee's Husband

I'd like to introduce you to my wife
Who's in the powder room. Her name's Renee.
She's beautiful but needs to live in strive
—Only with me, a charitable man.
Doctor, would you snitch a canapé
For me, by reaching over if you can?

Why should I suffer? When I was a child
My mother would always battle
Not with my father, not with my brother—*me*,
Though I never acted wild.
She'd holler when I'd shake my rattle,
Or suddenly shake me violently.

But I want to get back to my wife,
Doctor. As you'll see when you see her mood
Swings, swinging from bad to good,
She gives me no calm in my life
Which I need with a mother like that.
Do we choose our mates from the past,
Looking for love that can't last?
She's like an acrobat

Not in bed, but with emotions.
I want her on medication
—True Women's Liberation
From all her crazy notions
Of how I'm black and white, of how I

Deprive her, showering her with gifts.
She yells it is for *me* I give her little lifts,
And why don't I let her die?

* * *

Renee, come meet this fine psychiatrist.
I didn't catch your name at first.
Put that drink down. I insist.
Have a coke if you're "dying of thirst!"
These canapés are great. Aren't they Doc?

Not gin and tonic! Tell her it's no good,
On top of these ups for her mood,
To drink, that they'll put her into shock.
What she buys from these dealers is shlock!
It's better she mix food:
Liverwurst, frankfurters. Would
You bite them like you bite my cock!
What do you mean? He's used
To hearing words like this!
Tell him how you bite when we kiss,
When you're getting, like now, juiced.

* * *

Please, doc, don't wander off.
I know you don't like talking,
You guys—silent types who cough
Ahem, ahem. Don't start walking
Away from me, or else I'll give you you-know-what.
Don't stare like her who's cool.
Especially when I'm hot.
Don't treat me like an infantile fool
Who, when he's rattled, will shake.
I'm not the kind of man
Who'd rather bend than break
But will do everything he can.

Why am I talking like this,
When I'm asking for your assistance
To help my wife, not piss
You off with what she calls my butcher's persistence?
So here I've introduced you to my wife
Who's eating like she should to keep her health.
We'd like a consultation. Please, your card.
The fee's no matter. I'm a man of wealth.
Who'll pay what's necessary till this strife
Between us ends. You'll be her bodyguard
Because one day I'll go, I'm scared,
Out of control, if she keeps acting mad
At me, at what's inside her, at the wall
She always bangs when we're embattled,
When I act cool, when I call her on all
Her manipulations, when I refuse to get rattled.

* * *

Put that drink down. Where are you going?
A mood swinging her to that good-looking man.
Dance with him, bitch. Stand up if you can.
Do you see how she's showing
You, spitefully, how nuts she can be,
Deserting me like this,
Giving that stranger a kiss?
Look at what she does to me!

Renee's Dance Partner

Look at that Spanish guy in camouflage,
Those Calvin Klein fatigues and combat boots,
That beard trimmed in a mirror in the woods
Where Larry sends him whiskey and canned goods,
Like Larry's father stocked an Elks Club lodge

With little franks and long cheroots.
Why these phallic images, Doc?
Why am I fighting down an urge to tweak
A chin hair from that strutting, radically chic
Cartoon? Let's do, "She loves me, love me not"
On him, sprinkle this caviar with snot,
These slices of—that's this?—our Larry's cock?
You should have listened to the malice of
That quasi-nymphomaniac Renee,
The one whose husband riveted your ear.
She told me if you treated her, she'd play
With you with words; then where you fell in love
With her, she'd screw you to the wall with fear
Of suicide, malpractice, homicide
—Until I felt it bulging in my pants.
Isn't that weird? She knew, giggled,
Urged everyone to watch me dance.
I parodied a Charleston, till I wiggled
Into the bathroom where I jerked it down,
Thinking of Larry's girlfriend. Listen, Joyce
Is not the girl for him. She's smart, she's kind.
The only woman in this phony town
I ever loved, could love. And who's her choice
To give her inner riches to, to marry?
This 1960's throwback, little Larry.

I'll tell you now what's cooking in my mind,
And brings these little franks and Larry's cock
Together. Larry (You'll think this nuts)
In college had the hots for guess who? Crazy
Renee, the pom pom Queen, whose every honey
Was someone with a hoard of family money,
Like him the Meat King with his chopped meat putz.
Not sentimental Larry she called "lazy."
We'll dance again. But this time when we kiss,
Slipping a pill from mouth to mouth, I think
I'll tell her—leading her by the waist outside—

That the way to zap her husband for the shrink-
Sending he wants to do is to piss
Him off right now by taking Larry for a ride
In Meato's big back-seated Rolls (Un!) Royce
While I, in commotion, comfort Joyce.

The Old Maid

You're flirting with me, though I'm half-alive,
Trapped in a body turning forty-five.
I made those lines up, Doctor, like a guy,
Not to flirt, but to subtly ask you why
I'm at this party for this silly cause
When everyone I've met here so far bores
Me with their chatter, while their heads turn back
At every sexy twenty-year old snack.
What would you call them: Children? Pederasts?
Afraid of Time? Of anything that lasts?
I've put my years in on the couch (not bed),
Trying to leave a world inside my head
Of Family, Neighborhood—all crazy, yet
Much warmer than this world; this silhouette
Of business people, using work instead
Of family for a place to block their dread
Of isolation, like this party for
That Latin Marxist, womanizing bore.
What do you think his politics could be
When he's pinched each woman on the ass but me,
Only because I never turned my back
To him? These macho guys are gay, attack
The ass, afraid of what a woman can
Present. Deep down, I think, they want a man.
That's what this party's for—to celebrate
The revolution of that potentate
Over his constitution—which is gay.

Look at the way he mouths his canapé
While talking to that boy—is that Joyce's son?—
About artillery, the kind of fun
You have as they recoil and make a hole
To burrow in like some sex-crazy mole.
Is this what men don't want in me, my wit?
My realistic view of life? My grit?
There's nothing wrong with me except my age,
Our age we live in like our body's cage.
Doctor, if there were world enough and time,
We'd have no tragedies, no walls to climb.

* * *

What do I think of your guest, that Latin lover?
With good analysis, he might recover
The early motives of his need to kill.
No joke. I think he's seriously ill,
As everyone who makes not love, but war.
Without his jargon? Just a Conquistador.
Sorry you asked me? No? Then, listen, Larry.
Throw the next party for when you marry
Joyce, or for life, at least for food relief,
Not for this creep who brings us death and grief.
You know, you're also nearly forty-five.
It is miraculous to be alive
—Lonely or crazy, poor, rich, middle-class—
Wanting a piece of male or female ass,
Not this destroyer in his khaki slime,
This bore, this thief of other people's time.

* * *

What do you think of Larry? Should I ask?
Failed in some developmental task?
Maybe of separating from his mother,
So that he has a need to undercover

Merge with a stronger man to help him leave
The safety of her skirts? Am I naïve
In using psychoanalytic jargon? No!
I like your laugh, Doctor. Shall we gossip at
Each fool we see? Or would you rather chat
With someone younger, sexier? No crime
To want a newer packaging of Time.
You hear the way I deprecate myself,
A dusty bottle on a dusty shelf?
Empty except when I am feeling witty.
Beneath these battle scars, you know, I'm pretty.
Dust me off, I'll turn into a genie.
I used to call my analyst a meanie
When he looked trapped like that. And he was right.
I've got to run. Have a good time tonight.

The Guest Of Honor

Of course I know Dr. Struthers! Author of
Father and Sons, Macho Men/Their Mothers,
Two of the books I take into the hills
To teach my people how to bring out love
In what we call our sisters and our brothers.
I read aloud as we go through drills.

You look amused. Bewildered. Tell me what!
Señor, this isn't flattery. It's fact.
I've even read your esoterica,
Under a palm tree on an army cot
—That one on how we're doomed to re-enact
(All of us, not just the hysteric) "The

Death of mirroring Self-Objects." Have you read
McPhee's provocative biography? No?
His thesis is I'm driven to repeat
My father's being pummeled in his bed.

Each strategy repeats each murderous blow
Struck by his first son, adopted from the street!

Intriguing? Shall I stay in New York City,
On your couch, and put my actions into words,
With no assassin in the waiting room,
Until we find the psychic nitty-gritty?
—As doctors used to look in their kings' turds
For signs of self-destructiveness and doom.

Sorry for being light. McPhee cuts deep.
Down there you're taught to treat your wounds with action;
Food, food and more food when they sense my state
—Despair!—when they can't wake me up from sleep.
There's developing a Young Turk faction
Ready to destroy me—full of hate,

Full of macho turds to fill their emptiness,
Their empty mothers that they've got inside,
Frightened child-women who abandoned them,
Like mine... It's not too difficult to guess
The way she acted when my father died.
A son was something merely to condemn

Like the judge condemned my brother. She'd look
For signs of violence, madness in me, though
I was her own, though I had different genes.
I had to keep my nose pressed to a book.
If I was struck, I couldn't strike a blow.
The schoolyard joke! Later she'd check my jeans

For condoms, till I wanted to raise hell.
Oh, how I fucked and fought in adolescence
While she retreated more and more to prayer.
I justified my passion to rebel
By quoting Marx and Lenin, Che Guever-
"Ah! Ah! Ah! That's more the essence,"

You'd say in *Macho Men/Their Mothers*. But hear
The actor wants to take his makeup off!
I hate the ignorance of peasants. Food, more food,
This revolution to deny their fear
That God The Father's dead. Please, don't scoff
At my simplistic use of you. I brood

About my motives when I strategize.
I want to be free. *They* want to be red.
Illiterates and autodidacts, they
Quote me Marx, Lenin, while Communism dies
All over Europe! They want to get ahead,
Those bureaucrats-to-be, the proven way.

How can I live with my own fabrication?
How can I live freely, not revolted,
Not a tyrant to myself, not led
Into self-assassination?
Wouldn't Larry, that idealist, be jolted
If he could see the drama in my head,

The sacrificial rite that makes t.v.?
Since Our Father died, we need blood, more blood
—The Kennedys, Martin Luther King.
The final makeup they will do on me
Will simply be my face shoved down in mud,
My brothers and my sisters pummeling.

from
Ending the
Twentieth Century

from Manhattan Elegy: A Sequence

Manhattan Elegy

The past is like a library after dark
Where we sit on the steps trading stories
With characters we imagined ourselves to be.
Neighbors in clothing from our childhood stroll by,
Unmolested, nodding at us, benevolently.
One with your father's face tips his fedora.
You lower your eyes in shame. I look back.
Someone is sitting at a long table,
Reading in the moonlight. I must look startled.
He holds a forefinger to his lips
As if it is a candle for the dead.
You tap me on the shoulder and I turn back.
The street is dangerously empty
Except for the newsstand lit yellow,
Where your mother in a nightgown
Showing beneath her blue coat buys the *Times*,
A pack of *Kools* and, eyeing us, lights one.
You race to her, turn a corner. Goodbye.
I'm frightened, as if I am a foreigner
In a city under siege. Yet I know
It is still mid-century. Underground
Are only subways carrying boisterous
Party-goers or somber family men
Working the night shift or harmless bookies
Respectful of the No Smoking signs.
I walk to where the newsstand, shut,
Advertises brand names I'd forgotten.
I shove my hands into my pockets and whistle
A song we danced to when we were young.
I walk on for blocks, until I smell
Smoke from the burning borough of the Bronx.

Spring

At the Jefferson Memorial this Spring,
Cherry trees flamboyantly display their lesions.
Tulips announce in white and scarlet black
That they, like you, will only last a season.
You picnic barefoot with your dying friend
On macrobiotic citruses and grains.
You watch a mother with her noisy son
Fly styrofoam airplanes at surprising angles.
You wonder if this small domestic scene
That you derided wasn't what you always wanted.
Jefferson stands noble, safe, and bronze,
One of the celebrated dead you envy.
What would he wonder, looking down at you
This afternoon before the Middle Ages,
Helpless where a corrupted body politic
Matches a tragically infected people?
You gather up your detritus of peels,
Plastic containers, careful not to litter,
And look back frantic at what you might have been:
The boy and his mother curving their planes
Into never-again-seen Euclidian loops.
Time, says the virus in your bloodstream,
Time to go.

The Magic Kingdom

When we were young and optimistic, rich
In time, Main Street, U.S.A. seemed poor in soul.
Its rows of churchly, gingerbread houses,
Where clichés slept and fed, bored a poet
Who wanted us cynical as Paris
With its wise Sartre and sexy Signoret
Sitting in raincoats at *Les Deux Magots*
While a knowing Piaf number played.

Ah, my thick-haired boy, covering your bald spot
At the window of Main Street's Magic Shop,
While your son fingers a Kennedy half dollar,
Then makes it disappear, how did you like
The assassination of hope,
Your brutalizing war, your ugly tourists
—These conquering Japanese—
Visiting your childhood like a wax museum?

At the end of Main Street, Cinderella
Gray and menopausal waits in her castle.
She is singing the words of the Piaf song,
Non, je ne regrette rien. But she does.
She regrets everything and has learned nothing.
The tourists run in and out of her
Like an old tramp, despite her story above her archway,
Joking about the impotent Prince who never comes.

Parade

Wheeling down Main Street in technicolor light
Are Disney's heroes, our mythology,
A comfort in the middle of the night.

Mickey Mouse, Minnie, Uncle Donald, help.
The children of America are sick
Of AIDS, political hypocrites, and greed.
Snow White, Bambi, Lady and the Tramp,
It's midnight now, help us in our hour of need.

You helped us with the witch's ovens and
Her poisoned mushrooms. Goofy, Pluto, please.
Those childhood traumas were much worse than these.
Teach us to be courageous and naïve.

Spectacle

Out of the shtetl, out of pogrom
(My mother whimpering till America),
My son, nine, sits among macaws and hibiscus
At a white piano bar, handsome
As a movie star, smart as a physicist,
Ignorant (my doing) of his heritage.
We listen to a tinkling
Of T.S. Eliot's poems about cats,
Until my son yawns. It is getting late,
Near the end of a millennium.
The sky over Disney World is turning black,
The stars breaking through report light
From a time more primitive than my mother's era.
We leave the gentle fascist to his audience
And rise, American angels, in a glass
Elevator over the posh lobby
Of the hotel, with is three-story palms,
Its narcoticizing fountains.
I stretch out safe on the turned-down bed
And nibble the Godiva chocolates the maid left.
My son flicks on the end of a t.v. show
About a war orphan foraging
For roots in the Russian countryside. We watch
Until an artillery of fireworks
Begins bursting over the Magic Kingdom:
Red orange yellow blue indigo violet.
We kneel to watch between the bars of our balcony
As my mother, nine, kneeled behind a tombstone
And peeked out at the spectacle of her burning town.

Tell Me a Story

The photos haunt you from a gentler era,
The Eisenhower years you thought were boring,
Photos a corny uncle might have shown

While, as you'd put it, he did insurance whoring
In a small town tavern over beer.
You see a Southern football afternoon,
A mother sits beside the family Ford,

Hugging her daughter in a velour blouse,
A lace collar, a little pleated skirt.
The girl's face duplicates the mother's: kind;
Compassionate, unfortunately; alert.
Behind the Ford is a small suburban house.
What happens there is what you'd call "benign."

She sips her milk. She spoons homemade dessert.
The mother sits, her fists beneath her chin,
With nothing but her daughter in her head,
A future like America's: secure,
Confident, happy, certainly well-fed.
I hear you crying, "Pass the saccharine"
Years ago, "End this domestic tour.
Tell me a story, show me death instead."

I'll show the girl now grown to thirty-three,
In Central Park in autumn on a swing,
Pregnant in a plaid coat, scarf, beret,
Smiling at what the future's promising.
She's a pathologist, studies mortality
Daily. She is not naïve, but prey
To values you'd turn into posturing

—Like giving up a lucrative career
To help the poor, as you once tried to do.
Her door half-open while the night guard sleeps,
She stands, checking her messages in Bellevue,
Lifting her shirt, adjusting her brassiere,
Till the homeless man she would have pitied leaps
Behind her out of chaos, cloven-hoofed.

You put *The News*, like horror, gently down,
Fatigued by how fiction is daily fact.
You hate your shallow cynicism, sit
In your kitchen window-seat, reflect
On what brought catastrophe to this town:
Drugs, poverty, illiteracy, "bullshit
Liberal sentiment." All of that seems abstract.

You think of rituals, the sacrifice
Of virgins; in your own time, of the Jews
The Eisenhower years made people forget:
Washing the dishes, reading the local news
Of marriages and church bazaars, advice
From Dear Abby, ads for Bibles and bassinets.
You're wistful for morality, taboos.

You squint at the clockwork scene below:
The homeless sprawled, as if in alleyways,
The middle class aimlessly plunking quarters.
"Pedigrees," you smile, "among the strays."
You close your eyes as it begins to snow.
'You weep for the mother and her murdered daughter.
"*Où sont les neiges d'antan,*" you start to say.

Celebrating
for Dick Allen

I

To celebrate your turning forty-five,
We toured my past, where you had never been:
The 1950's Lower East Side, alive
With first and second generation Jews,
Poles, Ukrainians (like your wife Lori);
Each block a town, with flower boxes, clean,

Where you could cure pathology with art,
Where I first met my comic, street-wise Muse,
Playing the violin for a gang that jumped me.
I took her to my roof that summer night
And, while the city snored, she kissed and hugged me
And talked in double stops and won my heart.
Thus at Ratner's I began my history
While ordering a travelogue of food:
Cheese and blueberry blintzes, eggs, onions, and lox,
Kasha varnishkes, borscht, mushroom and barley soup
—Enough to keep off thoughts of our mortality,
As they kept me from scratching chicken pox.
The waiter, looking like his Jewish mother,
Eyes a traffic cop's held up his hand and smirked:
"Tell me, do you want your coffee perked,
Or just the beans with a side of boiling water?"
"I used to be the kid who fucked your daughter."
"I never had a daughter . . . What else?"
So I explained to you our being rude
Was just a tribute to our tenements, throngs
Jostling through pushcarts, haranguing on and on
About the union, poems of Glatstein, Schwartz.
Itinerent knife-sharpners.singing ghetto songs,
Gypsy musicians, horses wearing flowers,
Relics among the cars – as I am old
Among my memories...Where have they gone,
Those intricately living-in hours?

Avenue A has tiny pieces of quartz
Or mica in its concrete slabs. "We're flush!"
I joked as the sun struck immigrant gold.
But then I saw the rubble in the park
Where I would practice jump shots way past dark
And once outscored Russ Cunningham. "Who he?"
You asked, knowing if you asked that seriously,
We'd both be pained. "Like What's-his-name, the star
Of your unchanging Adirondack town."

Like some rejected lover trying to revive
Memories more for comfort than for passion's sake,
I called the ghost of Garfein's restaurant
From behind its boards. This was where plush
Weddings and bar mitzvahs enthralled the slums
Surrounding it—with spreads of caviar,
Scotch salmon, beluga sturgeon, where
My parents' generation foxtrotted, gallant,
Till after cake and coffee clasping hands,
Stamped the hora to Victor Goldring's band's
Alto and tenor saxophones and drums:
The notes now simply molecules of air,
As indistinctive as my mother's kiss.
You grinned, considered the lengthening ash
Of your cigarette, then flicked it in the trash
Heaped in front of Garfein's. "I can't reminisce
Like you, being a self-denying mystic
Whose life—and yours—are just parentheses
In Time, yours maybe more extravagant
With all your Lower East Side tumult, these
Boarded-up kosher catering halls,
These discount stores."
                "No, they were elegant.
You see the decorations on these walls,
That fortress of a building up ahead?
We lived there on the fourth floor." "Who's that, Fred?"
"Frieda Goldring? Victor's wife," I said.
"God!" A face drooped from stroke that once was tough.
"Remember me?" I asked.
                "I've had enough,"
She said, "of the indignities of age.
But I remember you on Victor's stage
At twelve with such a passion to create
With your fiddle only for the music's sake.
"Do you still play?" We both looked in the void
Where memory, then effort crumbles. "I hate

To say I don't But I write poems."
                              "Promise me, make
One of this place, one that can't be destroyed."

II

To celebrate my turning forty-five,
We slowly circled Thrushwood Lake, the scene
Of poems I knew by heart, but now alive
With your reciting—urgent mystical news
You divined from an ordinary story
Of a muskrat, willow, and a doctor lean-
Ing with his violin to finger Mozart,
While you were swimming sidestroke with your Muse
Of science fiction and philosophy.
You told me details of your soul's dark night
That you transformed into an allegory
About the future of the Sacred Heart.
These were the birthday gifts you gave to me
As we meandered through the willow wood,
Cautioning each other over icy rocks
Till, in a clearing, halved our age to scoop
Snowballs we smacked against a dying tree.
I broke a branch and traced a batter's box
And challenged, "Try to throw one past me, brother."
You kicked back, then exaggeratedly jerked
Into a windup, brushed me back, mock-smirked
As I mock-tipped into the freezing water:
"You know an aging poet gives no quarter!
You'll write carping confessions now—or else!"
"Oh? I will pin your ears, Decrepitude.
You'll write in academic free verse, little songs
Of life-long adolescent carryings-on
Of hippie days in Oriental ports
Where you sold drugs, draped girlfriends in sarongs
(Their Middle Western braids done up in flowers),

All Yuppies now, perfectly self-controlled,
Ironically recalling days long gone
Only when crocked, only at Happy Hours."
But then you gave the best of all retorts,
People Through The Train Window, "born to rush
Out on the earth and die." You sang of "old
Gravestones . . . mystic restaurants," familial dark,
As if we were standing at the opened ark
And *dawning* for Frieda's spirit. She
Was laid to rest with Victor "silently"
Only the night before (wasn't that bizarre?)
In New Montefiore, what's now my small hometown,
A violent place where nothing can survive
Except, as Frieda said, the poems we make.

But if our efforts aren't permanent,
If they are crumpled into that great hush
With Jim Croce's voice and Goldring's drums,
Among the molecules of Garfein's caviar,
Then what? You squeezed the freezing air
And cried, "Oh seize the day," exuberant
That you possessed *this* winter in your hands,
As if to say, "A mystic understands
What you couldn't notice in your busy slums."
But what about what Frieda made me swear?

When Time clicks shut its black parenthesis
Around Allen, Dick 1939 dash,
Will all our poems disintegrate to ash,
Even your masterpieces, even this
Passage I am writing now? Tell me, Dick,
Will everything be gone, your cry to seize
The day, this, that, that mystic restaurant
With all the Catholics, Muslims on their knees,
With Cohens pleading in their prayer shawls,
With Hari Krishnas madly jubilant,
With widowed Sufis shrieking caterwauls,
With all your dreams of histories ahead?

Will nothing keep of this poor Dick and Fred?
Even the echoes of the lines you said,
"Can we imagine that? All dead, all dead,
All of us dead who never lived enough?"
Oh no, dear friend, though sensitive we're tough
And, as we have survived our crazy age,
We'll talk forever this page with your page.

And so we nattered on to celebrate
My 45th, circling Thrushwood Lake
To find our families still alive, annoyed
We took so long, that we had made them wait
For me to wish upon my birthday cake:
    Once upon a time, we were overjoyed.

Underground Song

Authoritative in his blue MTA
Uniform, The Conductor opens subway doors
For bank clerks, beggars, salesman, dealers, whores
Jostling and cursing, going to hell each day

Under ads for face lifts, attack dogs, free
Trauma clinics, hotlines for crack addiction,
Numbing newspapers, escapist fiction,
Schools for Beauty—canvasses for graffiti.

The Conductor shouts, "For those of you depressed
Because you have been raped or simply mugged,
I'm gonna entertain you. I ain't drugged.
How many here passed your last AIDS test?

—Raise your hands . . . Get 'em up!" Some passengers do.
"What hairy hands there!" Now he's getting smiles.
"We're traveling for decades, not for miles:
Black, Italian, Irish, Polish, Jew.

Me? I'm half Manhattan, half a Presley.
'Whatzzat?' the lady's asking with her eyes.
I'm gonna show you nobody dies,
Not our heroes, not this city."

He sings two choruses of *Jailhouse Rock*.
The crowd bewildered giggles, shrugs, snorts, grins.
He flails his arms, he shakes his head, he spins
Singing, "Everybody in the whole cell block

Are dancing to the *Jailhouse Rock*." And they do.
The whole motley car, half of them high,
Are singing, rocking to this lullaby
Until the train stops. "For those of you

Going," he shouts, "to *Heartbreak Hotel*
Where you wake up half the night to screams,
Gunshots coming from windows or from dreams,
Remember Elvis loves you and be well,

In SRO's where no phone ever rings,
Where you cook dinner on a hot plate, where
You fall asleep to t.v. in a chair,
Remember, somewhere, New York City sings."

The Sundial

The frantic magic of your youth is gone.
How you lost it, only time can tell,
As stories take shape only near their end,
When the hero in a quiet house, alone,
Writes a letter to a near stranger
About his exploits history is forgetting:
The battlefield, the board room, and the rescue,
Speeches to uncomprehending children,
A handshake from a disgraced mayor.

With each line, the times, not he, diminishes.
He folds his letter like a paper crane,
Japanese magic, pure and sedentary.
Beside the letter is a bowl of petals,
His daughter's photo before she grew resentful.
He eases from his chair and surveys the room:
The furniture in sheets like cartoon ghosts,
The windows opened to the sunny garden
Where the past remains unchangeable in memory.
In his bravest moment, he walks out the door,
Leaves his key, the letter in the mailbox,
As you know, for you, tired of the board room,
Charmed by the plantings in the sunny garden,
The wicker furniture, the lazy talk,
The brochures of the Japanese vacation,
The papers with the details of the rescue,
The sundial with its motto *Time is Circular*.
He leaves the once familiar street. Come. Go.

Song of the Suburbs

The prospect of an automatic life:
Working from nine to five, dinner, then bed,
Maybe a night or two with the wife;
Watching t.v. or visiting the dead

Or fixing doorknobs or the sink on weekends.
That's what we rebelled against in youth.
We were going to fix the world, set social trends
In conscript dungarees. We possessed the truth.

And we did for a decade or two,
Until rejection and outrage wore us down.
Must I catalogue everything we foreknew:
The corruption of our country and our town?

Adolescents see things clearly, simply.
Though they reject us, outrage us, bless them.
Though we protest, we really are the enemy
Like our parents. Truth is, we depress them,

Cling to them like the future that is past
Or parents living only in our heads.
Rebel against yourself, iconoclast.
Let the living live, the dead be dead.

Earth Angel

Silence in the suburbs. Sleepers are tucked
Into green, opaque Monopoly houses
With their betrayals, cancers, bankruptcies
Poeticized in dreams that hold their soft
Three-pound brains, as a mother her nursling.
You who can't sleep without street noise
Sit in your car, listening to *Earth Angel*,
In The Still Of The Night, joyous fifties' songs
You brought home from junior high school.
Then you return, disbelievingly,
To your weary body approaching fifty.
You compare the trivia of your life
To the tragedies of two millennia.
Stranded, you yearn for mythic meaning.
You think of the Gaea Hypothesis,
Yow Earth is a single organism,
A pale blue Easter egg in the palm of God . . .
You start your motor, hoping to wake no one,
And ease slowly past the cemetery
Where your faceless parents lie.
You listen to the wee hours traffic
Helicopter report into Manhattan,
The reassuring sisterly voice
Chattering with the news of the relatives:

"Relatively quiet on the Major Deegan,"
Quiet in the Bronx where your grandmother lived,
Lighting candles, stroking, who cares? your face.
You turn into the service road past her house
—A crack den, a fox with AIDS in grandma's bed.
At a traffic light at the end of the road,
You stop out of middle class compliance
And a panhandler, your age, washes your windshield.
You hand him a five dollar bill he "rips"
—A fifties' joke between you. You watch him
Rush to McDonald's for a dawn breakfast
And remember your father prodding you
At 4 A.M. to eat onion rolls and carp at Ratner's
Before you went fishing, before you fled
To the suburbs, in a time, it seems,
Before time.

The Poet to His Younger Self

So there you are: twenty, hands on your hips,
Squinting at the sun. Dressed in a white shirt
And purple cashmere sweater, you sniff the Spring air
For death, merely to write a poem about it.
Your wife-to-be takes your hand.
                                      You stroll into the woods:
A mythological creature, half man
Half woman, dappled under the leaves
Like the checkered tablecloth you spread.
Nothing to trouble you but the bees. You read
Keats to her. She hears nothing but your voice.
You read well. You say you're innocent
And must suffer to write well, but don't know
What that means, don't know the *ubi sunt* theme
Is serious. You are so serious.
She tickles you, plays hide-and-go-seek in the trees.
Counting to fifty, you think of me

Thinking of you, imagine that I mourn
Nothing, not myself, not the real deaths of friends.
Play, children, unnoticed under the leaves.

The Lake

The lake is always here for you,
Especially at sunset, near
The end of a millennium:
Its surface cobbled brownish blue,
Its docks of dark aluminum,
Its sailfish, poised to disappear.

Journal of the Plague Year

At other times, a small domestic scene—
The aftermath of dinner in our country house:
My son cuddling my wife in a religious haze;
The table between us strewn with steak,
Half drunk glasses of burgundy, a china bowl
Flecked with corn, its Vermeer spoon
Reflecting light from a Revere chandelier.
Meandering I sketch this in words
—Like an Impressionist.

Slowly our precious apparent Easter egg
Daylight purples, then succumbs to black,
And the cracked, primordial university reveals itself.
Still, back in the kitchen, *The Jefferson Starship*
Lustily sing "Homeward Bound" on the radio
And a trinity of deer tiptoes
Through the apple orchard.
They watch me in my artificial light,
Confident I will let them eat their fill.

A Letter to Friends

Creatures of love, we put our dead away
Sleepily, with no strength, no appetite,
Until we rouse ourselves to reminisce,
As if we're lighting a favorite play.

So the eighteenth-century put away their wigs,
Moles, powder, buckles, and brocades
And stilled their bows and closed their harpsichords,
Death shushing all their masquerades.

While we are mourning we appreciate
The momentary splendor of our lives,
The richness of our smallest interactions
With lovers, parents, children, husbands, wives.

Then maybe because we clearly see our fates
On newscasts, in a stalled wailing ambulance,
In the mutilated offerings on our plates,
We lose our frightening acuity in work.

When Renee died her best friend baked all night.
Hoping for hope, praying for faith, Fran stared
At her defunct fluorescent bulb and cried,
"Renee, give me light, give me your light."

Instantly the bulb began to flicker, then
It flared while Fran giddily baked,
As by my sister's Yahrzeit candle, she
Casually moves my pen.

My dears, this world, this illusion which in youth
Seemed permanent will, as the eighteenth-century
Become a litter of books, costumes, art,
Barely evocable, cannibalized truth.

Yet and yet and still yet Fran's miracle
Tells another truth which in panic we obscure
With manic masquerades, until we're struck
By Death, as the clock strikes. Of this I'm also sure.

Fin de Siècle

In your moonlit dining room,
Near the end of two millennia,
You sit among your photos, in wonder
And fatigue. Standing at two
Near the Russian baths, you and grandpa
In t-shirts, *shvitzing*, while your mother
Upstairs weeps over the news from Europe.
Then a moment later, you alone, mustached and grinning,
Hoisting your infant son, thinking of the year
Two Thousand,
A fantasy you thought would never come.
You squint into the darkened kitchen,
Where a radio you hadn't noticed plays,
"Over and over and over again, my friend,
You don't believe we're on the eve of destruction."
Reluctantly you get up and flick the lights on
And change the station to an earlier era,
Where *The Penguins* sing in your adolescence:
Earth Angel, Earth Angel, will you be mine,
My darling dear, love you all the time."
Surprised by tears, you close your eyes
And see the long-dead standing
Above Earth's corona, *Mom, Dad*
In nightgown and pajamas, calling to you:
Do you remember me, what do you remember,
What's happened in the past decade, how's your son,
How's your wife, how's your sister's cancer,
How is your car running, how does it feel

To be middle-aged, how is The Cold War,
How is Manhattan, your blood pressure,
Are the Jews safe, do you have good teeth
Which chatter in a skull, how is your nerve
Facing the next stage: age, illness . . . ?
Now the news is playing, mosquitoes spiral
In the lamplight. Rain splatters the porch,
Crickets rub their legs, the window fan whirrs,
Earth whirrs silently and slowly; then the news ends,
We are all safe, then a storm report . . .

from Creature of History: A Sequence

Daydreaming

You contemplate a European Lake
Where picnickers enact a comedy
Of Aryan romance: an ingenue

Eludes a subtle pass a soldier makes;
A chunky salesman, drunk and oniony,
Gooses a widow as she'd dishing stew.

You're spooning chocolate mousse or German cake,
Enjoying temporary sanity.
You see the agony awaiting you,

The nightmare when the 20th Century wakes
Amidst the litter of this bourgeoisie.
You see this as an analyst and Jew.

It doesn't matter what discoveries you make
About the psyche and its history.
Time and the world will have its way with you.

Yet, for a moment, the future is opaque.
You're laughing with your living family.
The day is sunny and the lake is blue.

Gravedona

Lost in Gravedona without a map,
You ask directions in handicap
Italian of a stout old woman.
She laughs, "Stop Struggling, come in,
And whilst I think them out, I'll make us tea

And, if you don't mind, have a chat with me,
For I'm half-Welsh, half-Genovese."
Her father built this house, planted trees
"That will outlive this century. I'll bore
You, maybe, nattering about the war.
I need to take the rust off of me tongue,
Living as I do among young
People who take up German. Whoosh, it makes me boil,
Me who dieted on castor oil.
So," she smacks her stomach, "me bag is packed,
Time's refugee, ready to be attacked."

She waddles to the kitchen to make tea.
You ease into her affability,
Scanning her knickknacks, cheap paperbacks
(*Charles and Di*), miniature Union Jacks,
Photos of The Pietà, her son:
No, her husband, arms crossed with a gun.
"That's right, like me he was a Partisan
Hid in these hills. They tortured him, poor man,
When a spy, born in this town, gave him up."
She pours the tea, then hot milk in my cup.
She spots the admiration in my eyes.
"Pettiness survives, heroism dies.
Isn't that so in The States?"
                              "Sure
We've lost our confidence with our naiveté.
We've given up what Hitler couldn't take.
Grinning, she slices a home-baked cake.
"During the war, fat me was the head
Of the Resistance here. I baked the bread,
I bought the boots... Yes, in Dongo, I
Helped capture Mussolini. Heels to sky
He hung, a creature out of Dante's Hell.
I'll die with many stories I could tell.
Unlike you, young people here don't care
About the blood and terror in the square

They drink their coffee in. It's only we
Who are afflicted with this history:
Hitler, Goebbels, Goering—facts and names,
Heroes now in children's video games.
Just Once Upon A Time And Long Ago."
Her eyes begin to close. It's time to go.
"Tea finished already? You'll want your map.
I've traced it. Seems I can't resist me nap,
Journeying to a better world I knew.
You've not too far to go. Here's luck to you."
She clicks her cup against my empty cup.
"Hail and farewell," she grins, "and bottoms up."

The Seduction at Villa Carlotta

Nature is never wrong, the lilies say,
Simply alive in the pond, life goes on.
Despite carnivorous violence, firestorms,
We are porcelain quiet. Sit on this bench,
Listen to The Baroque Ensemble play
Music composed during the French
Revolution; cherish the bees
Closed in those petals, close your eyes,
Close them, close yourself in these harmonies.
All civilizations die.

Stresa—the Borromeo Islands

Since you read Stendhal, Flaubert, De Musset,
Isola Bella seemed a hazy dream:
Ramparts of gardens rising out of water,
Water nymphs stunned into statuary,
Grottos where walls of pebbles and mortar
Formed sea shells and sea creatures,
Rooms with mandolins and *violas d'amores*,

Balustrades where assignations were made
With a nod, a wink, the snap of a fan.

All was true enough, as the German guide
Declaims in gutturals: This was the conference room
Of Ramsay MacDonald and Mussolini.
Here Napoleon slept and stepped outside
To sniff dahlias and rhododendrons.
There in that maze of midget hedges
Peacocks and cardinals mixed, flaunting their plumage.
History, like this baroque estate,
Was mere fantasy: Nazis and Popes,
Servants and lizards, water nymphs and devils,
As in the puppet theater before the grottos
Where a procession of townspeople
Display the Deadly Sins that shaped their faces.

You unfold the *Herald Tribune* under your arm
And stare at the photo: "*Four Decades Later
Lithuanians Delve Into History.*"
A woman in a babushka and flowered frock
Weeps over a skull she cradles in her hands,
"*Plucked from a mass grave dug in Stalin's terror,
Or in World War II.*" The guide squints as if you held
A relic, then turns back to joke
About the statue of, "A Chinaman
Two centuries old, *forse*, Mao Tse-tung."

The crowd laughs as if they've lived forever
And moves on to the outdoor amphitheater
Black and gray in the sunlight, its gardens
Cemeterial, its statuary
Looking past Stresa where Mussolini fled
And the crowd, mindful of history, caught him
By the heels in Dongo, till he swung
Like the pendulum of a Borromean clock.

The Coup

For the first time in years, you're really lost,
Provoking a fight-fight with a foul
Venetian boatman who's blown smoke near your son's
Face, though your wife's shown him *Mucosolvan*
And you've shouted *Congestivo!* You know
Only afterwards, when the trance is over, when your son
Tells you he was scared, you've really lost
Yourself; so you sit alone, late at night
In the hotel's garden, sipping *vino rosso*
And thinking how this trip, repeats
Despite all you know, different aspects of
THE PRIMAL SCENE ... trade talk ... better left alone ...

At midnight, in the privacy of the garden
Behind Desdemona's Palace, your wife
After your son's asleep comes down to help you:
You talk about your self-analysis,
How, too late, the whole drama of your life,
The exposition set and nearly fixed
In infancy, is finally coming clear
When you've both worked hard and desperately need
To rest. You apologize, explain
How in the unconscious time doesn't exist,
Anymore than it does in Venice
—Where there in a palace window
 Flickering with television light,
A man, pacing, watches Gorbachev betrayed,
While in a street away, twisted and dark
As the mind's convolutions, Othello plots
To kill a ghost, his faithless mother ...

You put your glass down and take your lady's hand
And walk out front to the street
Where Mozambiques, hounded through Europe,

Hawk fake Fendi bags, fake Izod shirts,
Their torment all visceral, for the moment
More real.
   In just two generations, you think,
Your grandson, maybe affluent as The Moor,
Will find himself in a trance in a street,
Nose to nose, ready to kill or be killed
When he craves peace, is starved for peace.
You think the whole world's engineered like this:
On the large stage politicians playing
Scenes of their infancy, multitudes
Sleepwalking into battle, children screaming,
Children murdered, children dying of *kwashikor,*

While upstairs asleep in the lighted room protecting him
Your son turns your actions to metaphor,
Dreams of two knights, maybe his size,
In armor he's seen in the Doge's Palace,
Standing in a trance with ridiculous swords,
Tourists aghast at them.
     You take out a ten
Thousand lire note and hand it to the tall
Dusky entrepreneur smoking nervously.
He hands you a purple shirt with a green
Alligator near the heart you know is fake.
This is the best and only life you have,
The best you can manage. You take your wife's hand
And walk to Piazza De La Fenice
Where, posted on the opera door, *Otello*
Opens the Fall Season.

     You grin and walk to the bridge
Under the house where Mozart lived as a child
Touring Europe, his brain inexplicably
Teeming with beautiful escapes. Below
On the obsidian black waterway
The gray shade of a gondola

Slips by you; then the bridge is still
Except for you and your wife; then, from some other street
Or century, a woman sings *Così Fan Tutti*,
Passionately, unabashedly, pure.

Venice Spontaneous

The crowd at Piazza San Marco is listless, dark
Though it's a cool bright night, and the musicians
At Café Quandi are playing *Ave Maria*
With such luminosity, they bring tears to a Jew's eyes.
But the world, at least in Venice, these
Variegated tourists: Germans, Brits,
Japanese, Lebanese, Israelis,
Are hostage to mid-twentieth century *Zeitgeist*,
Like Gorby ("Is he dead?" "Is the Cold War Ready to resume?"), when a fat
Old woman (from Gravedona?) wearing headphones
Begins to shout in English: "The Coup
Is over, the ice has melted, wildflowers bloom
All over Europe, listen to the news!"
We do, this whole U.N., while Russians
In Lubyanka Square are dancing,
Dancing! Lifting Yakovlev aloft:
"Down with the KGB!" we shout. "Up with *perestroika*!"

On that note, the band at Café Florian
Strikes up a tune from a Bond film
—*From Russia With Love*.
                              The crowd roars.
Then *The Star-Spangled Banner*, and the crowd
Solemnity applauds. But then, when they play
John Lennon's *Imagine*, the crowd
In American jeans and cockamamie accents
Bursts into song. The Lebanese
Points at the crescent moon. The old

Woman grabs my hand and grins
In recognition. The Israeli in a *keepah*
Dips a tall German blond in a foxtrot.
My son whirls his yo-yo:
                         red, white, and blue
In "Around The World." Then someone
Throws a bouquet of roses down
From the Campanile, and a small
Girl (Russian?) catches it.

Then the bank plays a tune
Comically with a wide vibrato and
A pounding brass hand
—*"It's The Internationale!"*
And the old woman, drunk on victory,
Points at the lights coming from the ferry
Coming from the Lido, at teeny halos
The children make out of green
Florescent tubes, and the crowd
Raises their fingers: *Peace*.

Peasant Carts
    for Roger Hecht

Late at night in Wengen, in the Alps,
Exhausted after a day of hiking,
Somehow I'm thinking of you, vividly
Reciting your poems, regaling me with arcane
Tidbits of history, ignorant of how
The world has changed just so, how the Cold War
Which would never end is over, three
Mere years after your death.
I'm very tired tonight, Roger, and can't
Grasp how you are merely ashes,
How you suffered a ridiculous death

Hitting your head on the tub, those brains,
That gift, splattered, like some Croat's
By some Serb's, those brilliant poems
Out of print, and you stoic, cheerful, brave,
I suppose like Boris Yeltsin, but not grandiose
On a tank on the stage of history;
Just alone, hostage to illness, mute
After a while to your Muse.
                                      Church bells ring
In this clean and ordered hamlet, ring
All over Eastern Europe which, when you last looked,
Was entrapped like you in your dark room,
Your books, small briefs of history,
Protecting you, scripts for dramas
Like this tragic-comic *putsch*
—How you would have laughed at it,
At these inept drunken bureaucrats
Scurrying over the Kremlin, sliding their name
Tags into office doors their betters used,
Squabbling like peasants come to market
Poking each other, their carts full of nuclear bombs,
Bumping over dirt roads, terrified and alone.

Trümmelbach

A typically Swiss German, typically neat
Valley of chocolate houses with red
Raspberry flowerboxes and toy trains,
And cable cars and Heide and Julie Andrews
Dancing among the clean sheep on the vast
Almighty mountain peaks and, almost audible,
Yodeling and glockenspieling and lieder
Singing and church bells ringing: *Peace
For Chrissakes, peace*. In this
Typically Swiss German, typically neat
Valley, you stand before *Trümmelbach*,

Meaning *Streams like Drums*, before
Slopes covered with wildflowers and harp string grass,
Beneath cloud-untrammeled, serenely blue sky.
Trümmelbach, the name resonates
With romantic pomposity as you ascend
The mountain's rectum in a steep dark
Cable car, squeezing your wife's hand, your son's hand.
Trümmelbach, into whose bowels
The Monch, Eiger, and Jungfrau pour
Twenty thousand tons of glacial detritus per year.
Trümmelbach, where all boundaries are broken,
The ancient hidden shit-world of Europe,
Hitler's kingdom, the fury behind the borders
Of the Swiss dour face. *Trümmelbach,*
The bursting ethnic borders of Yugoslavia,
Of the fake Russian Empire: Georgia,
Armenia, Moldavia, Azerbaijan.
Trümmelbach, Trümmelbach, Streams like Drums.
You walk from one bellowing waterfall,
Small Niagras, to another, slipping, clutching the guard rail,
Staring in terror and awe, *Che Bella,*
Grand, Merveilleux, Sieg Heil!—*Trümmelbach.*

Creature of History

But for the Russian Revolution,
You wouldn't exist, not you whose mother fled
Kamenets Podolsk, nor your wife whose father fled
Moscow, nor your happy American son.
Now while it comes to an end, you sit
High over Zurich in a five-star
Hotel bathtub, sucking mangos, listening
To Tchaikovsky's Violin Concerto,
Played by Shlomo Mintz. Tomorrow
You will return to a country where some
Hunger for the simplicity of its old ideals,

Others, like thirties Communists, control culture,
And still others, racist
Politicians and street thugs, threaten
Pandemonium. You don't
Want to go home, you want
To go to Moscow, you want
To look up Gorby, visit relatives
Whom Stalin or Hitler missed.
What a century! What a creature of history you are,
Controlling the tub water with your big toe,
Hot, cold—like Gorby, befuddled,
Trying to relax, not in his dacha, but
In Moscow, getting up slowly so he won't slip,
Drying his chest, his tush, his head.

Survivor

Hid from Death, you collapse
Into your father's armchair,
As if in his arms, and ease
Into the timid wisdom of middle age.
You stare at your fruit trees where deer nibble,
At the soft autumn sky, its cirrus clouds
Drifting harmlessly as a child's thoughts,
At your carefully tended perennial garden
And abundant grape arbor and clipped lawn,
Thinking how illusory you are,
How shock weakens and repeated shock exhausts,
And how, despite our knowledge and best intentions,
Death repeatedly commits mayhem,
Private and public, as in the newspaper on your lap
Where Serbs slash breasts of women they've raped,
Burn their children, castrate their husbands . . .
You look away. Over the pine trees, your pine trees,
A hawk lifts a screaming rabbit in its claws,
Spiraling higher and higher into abstraction
Like the numbers of dead in the newspaper

Or the death-toll of your extended family:
Mother, father, sister, uncle, aunts
Who lived with you and had real names,
Who sat laughing with you over pot roast
And potatoes, red wine, and ginger ale
In that mythic kitchen in your childhood home.
Someone else's childhood. You look down at faces
Made of newsprint—shocked faces, grieving faces,
    accepting faces,
At cities like yours, sane in their architecture,
Efficient and health-conscious, except for the clouds
Of artillery smoke and gigantic Death,
Stepping between office towers, his machete
Real, sharp, relentless, indiscriminate

Hawaii—Drifting to the Volcano

Orphaned, aging, having no savings, and
No gods but Luxury to protect you,
Drifting with no thought, nothing to understand,
As Heraclitus said, from pool to pool,

From man-made cave to mane-made waterfall,
Past chaise lounges where Japanese read
Cheap American novels, past volleyball
Matches between screaming Germans and neutral Swedes,

Past cliffs off which French and Thai
Children grab knotted ropes and swing
Wide and high, shouting as they jump, *"Banzai!"*
You watch them drowning and resurfacing.

Then tired from relentless sun, you stop
Drifting, and breaststroke till you reach
"The Volcano Snack Bar," where you prop
Your elbows on a ledge. You glance back at the beach

Where our wife waves at your surfing boy.
You watch Italian honeymooners kiss,
Hear a tennis bum and matron comparing *poi*
To condoms—he is L.A., she is bluntly Swiss.

You're amazed at how such ethnic types seem free,
And unafraid of freedom, fearless of time
In which they bask in sunscreen. Thirsty
For hope, you order Perrier with lime

To toast them. But from the bar, CNN
Telecasts the world beyond this world cut down to size
—Bosnian prisoners reduced to skeletons
With nearly Jewish, disbelieving eyes.

A Muslim woman whispers how a Serb
Made her teenaged son lay his precious hand,
His right hand neatly on a curb,
Then chopped off his fingers, tore off her wedding band

And raped her. "Soon, you'll have a Chetsik boy,
Strong who will protect you, not like him
Who watched me take you like the Greeks sacked Troy."
The honeymooners, giggling, run for a swim.

Now German neo-Nazis deprived of Jews
Are beating up Albanians and Turks.
The matron asks her waitress to change the news.
But the news won't change. Even here evil lurks

Behind the waterfall, inside the cave.
Everyone knows that, tries not to see or hear
For a few days of truce. You toast them all, you wave
To your teenager striding the waves. "To us, mere

Creatures of History. Here's to Creation,
Though the same absurdist play or Passion Play

Repeats itself in every generation!"
That much is clear to you, downing your Perrier,

Ready to drown, resurface, drift in time.
You push off from the ledge and close
Your eyes. "Banzai!" This is the sublime
Fin de Siecle extravagance. You doze.

from

Time: New Poems

Hurricane

The eye becomes Manet's or Debussy's
On this inch-thick lawn facing the beach
Where blue and white casabellas match
The white-capped-green-to-nearly-cobalt sea

Held momentarily by swayback palms,
Miniature hills of purple heart-shaped flowers,
Bathers in hammocks skimming magazines
Describing black markets in nuclear arms,

And Polynesian waitresses bearing drinks,
Teenagers racing for kayaks, unperplexed
By the surf rising from the hurricane coming
Tomorrow or the next day or the next.

Highway of Cheap Love

> "On Saturday nights, as many as 300 young
> Women line the margins of E55, a Czech
> Highway near the German border...
> They speak a babel of languages: Czech,
> Romanian, Bulgarian, Hungarian, German.
> But they have only one thing to sell: sex.
> For the truckers and migrant workers who
> Ply the main road between Berlin and Prague.
> This particular seven-mile stretch of E55 is
> The "Highway of Cheap Love," the longest
> Brothel in the world, a smorgasbord of lust."
>
> (TIME)

I write this letter to you, fellow soul,
Degraded by this crazy human race,
As my daughter was on highway 55
A neighbor saw her looking half-alive
In wobbly high heels, rabbit stole
Plopped on her shoulders, rouged as if punched in the face.

She wanted to become a singer, dancer, though
She trained in the Budapest Ballet.
They simply called her "Swan," she had such grace,
Those quickening steps, that earnest open face.
And how she'd rush to kiss me in the morning, so
Gentle, trusting—"Swan!"—not that gypsy's prey!

The tragic flaw is mine. After my wife died
We hid, huddled inside. I never let
My angel truly light in Hungary.
I see her sunlit with her rosary
—That image makes me think of suicide—
I see her sitting in her window... Yet

The boy was handsome and romanced her
In the old high way of love—not 55!
Candlelit supper, gypsy violin . . .
I argued with her, but he took her in.
She'd be a European singer, dancer!
The Queen Bee stolen from his drone's dead hive.

I worked so many hours for her lessons, left
No energy to write my poems. Oh, I'm clever.
Radnoti's widow thinks my efforts "great."
It shames me I've no strength left to create.
Miklos wrote waiting to be shot, bereft
Of love, not poetry, of losing her forever.

I found your name and address in a book
Of poets in America, and hope
You take the time to do what I request:
Please reproduce her photo; that's Budapest
Winking behind her, welcoming as her look
—Cherubic then, rouged only by soap.

Above her face write something to cause pain
In those unfeeling travelers you know,
Those who might pass a lighted window (such
As I've passed many times) and start to touch
The girl inside, those who might sip champagne
Chilled in some Chad or Thai bordello.

They beat the girls or drug the girls, and take
Away their passports and their will. They're passed
Like currency until their value's gone.
Please reproduce her face for every John
You know. Enough—because my hands begin to shake.
During The War her grandparents were gassed,

Hidden by Catholics, I grew into eyes
That should have taught my daughter how to blink!

I needed something innocent and fresh.
Not *Europe*! She's gone the way of my family's flesh.
For fifty years we tried to civilize
Europe!—that rouged, that perfumed corpse, that stink.

Escape

Each day I have to wrestle with the dead,
The damaged ones who couldn't help themselves
But live maliciously inside my head.

I'm sitting in Hawaii with my wife
On a lanai, sipping herbal tea,
Watching the pattern of a better life

In the earthly paradise below me:
Seven iris-colored swimming pools
Vacuumed by boys erect with puberty,

Flexing muscles for the girls who pass
On rope bridges, tiled paths, down water slides,
Their inner lives all breasts and legs and ass,

And all around them tall sinuous palms
Ginger, plumeria, birds of paradise,
Overseen by a Bronze, fishing net in his arms

Flung toward the Pacific Ocean
Where surfers wait for wind and sailboats idle
And the girls massage themselves with suntan lotion.

I almost can immerse myself in this,
And let my precious and abusive dead
Rest in peace with self-analysis

—That lifelong struggle toward reality,
Like the bronze, muscular fisherman's
Contained and endless gesture at the sea

Which like the mind's unfathomable abyss
Houses a dark poetry, a shelled music,
Nourishing when opened, as a soul kiss.

Mosaic

1. Jews

<u>Your hat on backwards in a t-shirt, jeans</u>
<u>Slung low, as if you're trying to act black,</u>
<u>And Russian student rimless glasses</u>
<u>Like my father wore reading *The New Masses*</u>
<u>—Nonsense he made me study in my teens—</u>
<u>Another kind of Jewboy out of whack.</u>

"So, you've come to interview me for your book,
Your Ph.D. On 'race relations.' Good!
In the U.B.A.! (United Balkans.) We're
Going to *shmooze*, try to speak without fear,
Though one of us is deaf. From your shy look
I know your bias. Welcome to the 'hood.

"My name is Martin Abel, I'm a Jew
In hypocritical America's
Crown Heights, where self-righteous and benighted blacks
Like White Knights from the KKK, black Cossacks
(*Speak quietly*) did what they always do.
They found some Jews and acted murderous.

"My son says if I want to speak, calm down.
When Rodney King, a criminal but black,
Was beaten by six cops, I was appalled,
Disgusted, outraged, disbelieving, galled
The jury did not punish the attack.
From Crown Heights to Koreatown

"People screamed for a new trial, all of us.
And so, because the victim King was black,

Cops were convicted over his Civil Rights.
We all applauded, Jews like other whites.
But who screamed about justice for the pack
That mauled, and nearly kicked to death, that tedious

"White trucker who drove into the riot
After the cops were first convicted? That too
Was on t.v. Who screamed for that non-black,
And who screamed 'Justice' for the pack
That set upon this white Australian Jew,
This foreigner so modest and so quiet,

"This Yankel Rosenbaum, here to research
The Holocaust? Remember how, after the accident
In which a Hasid swerving killed a child,
A black boy Gavin Cato, people when wild,
How kids, parishioners from a bigot's church,
Rioted, trying to find where the driver went?

"Speak slowly, quietly, be understood,
Speak like a Jew, use neither gun nor fist.
The cops, afraid the driver had no chance,
Put him, panicked, in a Hasid ambulance.
The word spread quickly through the neighborhood
That cops helped the Jewish motorist

"Into the ambulance and shut the doors
On the boy. Blood libel! *Jews shut the doors. Kill
A Jew, kill the Jew, kill a motherfucking Kike.*'
Ready to party, gleeful, ready to strike,
They found their Jew and drove him to all fours.
They stabbed, discovering an ancient thrill

"Until his white face turned to *Yahrzeit* wax.
At first defying the New Hypocrisy
Out mayor came to sit at Yankel's side,

Then left relieved, not knowing that he died.
Unslaked, this mob, contemptuous of facts,
Thirsted for Jews, for days their lunacy

"Going unchecked, on orders from the top:
The black police commissioner, the black
Mayor. *You* tell me why. I call it a pogrom.
You would not call it that? I will stay calm
Despite the fact we could not find a cop
To help us when we suffered *our* attack,

"When screaming *'Kill the Jews'* they whacked my son
Deaf, the day he turned seventeen-years-old.
They broke his teeth, my teeth, my ribs, my soul.
Out of the shadows of history, a hole
In Hell they came, believe me, having fun,
Like Russian peasants, as our *bubbas* told.

"They caught one killer (You won't know the name),
Put him on trial. They jury set him free,
Then went out celebrating with Guess who?
The defense attorney! *'Fuck the dirty Jew!'*
Speak quietly. I'm doomed to live in shame.
I couldn't save my son from savagery!

"America will pay for cowardice,
For moral rot, this New Hypocrisy.
Speak quietly, we've got no Civil Rights,
According to the media, we whites,
When bigotry is reversed. Most whites don't piss
Blood like me. In our moral bankruptcy

"No one worries New York City will burn
In Jewish rage, that Jews will loot or kill,
Or even holler, Kill a black, Kill a *coon!*
But retribution will be coming soon

From God or history. We'll have our turn
With Sodom, Rome, with Germany, we will!

"So, for this interview, I'd like to close
In what, young man, I see in you,
Since what I see is most important for
The balance in your book. You nod. I abhor
Your coming here in the latest rage in clothes,
Not rage for what has happened to the Jew.

"There are always Jews like you, politically
Correct, left-wing assimilationists
Championing everyone's rights but yours,
Self-righteous, bloated academic whores,
Selling their souls for tenure. What I see
Is right on! Morally, you're full of twists.

"My son is saying with his hands I speak
Like a demagogue, that I'm sounding paranoid
And stereotype you for your clothes and looks.
What is the use of all your books
On race relations, when you've destroyed
Our moral base with realpolitik?

"And so, dear Jew, I'll show you to the door
And hope no riot out there catches you,
As maybe in the Pale of Settlement
It caught your *bubba*. Yes? Your argument
I've heard for centuries—on self-defeat.
I'm one kind, you're another kind of Jew."

2. *Go Down Moses*

You're here to interview me for a book
On race relations in this tragic place

—Crown Heights, or Bosnia, it's all the same.
I'm Sarah Moses, you may use my name.
I'm fifty-seven, of the human race.
I'm fat and blowsy and I love to cook

For all my grandchildren but one,
The one I think you came to see me for.
But we won't use his name because he'll get
Killed by a mob screaming, "Never forget!"
I lost one daughter who became a whore,
Who gave her momma Anthony, her son.

I brought my baby up on discipline.
He got all A's and starred in basketball
And loved his Grandma Moses, loved her cooking,
And told me brashly I was still good-looking.
Those seconds out there made no sense at all!
How can I tell you? Where shall I begin?

You know the details of that riot, when
A boy died in an auto accident,
When neighbors, people that we thought we knew,
Ran screaming through the streets to kill a Jew
Until they found this Jewish innocent
And acted more like rabid beasts than men.

For three nights they terrified Crown Heights.
I thought that I would have a heart attack
When out my window who did these eyes see
With a mob of hoodlums but my Anthony
Kicking a Jewish father in his back
While his frail boy screamed, *screamed* until the lights

Went out on him. I grabbed the baseball bats
Anthony saved with autographs of the Mets:
Carter, Strawberry, Keith Hernandez, Gooden.

My hands around the bats, my heart was wooden,
I ran out swinging, screaming ruthless threats.
They backed off snarling like a pack of rats.

Anthony used to sleepwalk as a child,
Looking for Daddy in his momma's bed,
The father he would come to call "No Face."
He has no quarrel with the Jewish race.
Something snapped on, then off inside his head.
He squinted at me and his eyes looked mild.

He looked in horror at the bloody pair
And ran for blocks, for months. For years
You mind a boy, think you know him, all
His darkest thoughts, you can't sleep trying to recall
Some incident with Jews. Nothing appears,
No image, words. All night you stare

At the clock, at his picture, at your palms.
You hear that high-pitched screaming, "I can't hear!"
You hear the father screaming, "Help him, please!"
You fall down broken on your Christian knees
And listen to his sobs like fire alarms
And watch him kiss his baby's bloody ear,

Watch in horror, watch him in disbelief,
And holler "Anthony!" down the empty street,
Then trudge my fat and weary body up these stairs,
Muttering what I think are Yiddish prayers,
Making up words, making something to eat,
Then plop down in misery and grief

In the chair you're sitting in. till the sun
Smears the window like a drunken face
Is smeared with blood. When you come to write
Your learned prose about the murderous night
And try to understand this thing called "race"
Or why these boys looked like they were having fun,

Remember that in every place on Earth
Victims turn to villains, conscience seems
The blinking of a New York City pigeon;
Unless we keep the strict laws of religion,
It means no more than our prophetic dreams
Or memories of Heaven at our birth.

I'm silly now and philosophical.
I have no insight, just a baseball bat
And knowledge that there's evil and there's good,
That I did everything a grandma could.
I'm just simplistic, aging, old, and fat,
And miss my baby—he was comical,

Parading in my hats or provoking me
Or tickling my feet or making me listen to rap
Or root for the Mets though they'd lose game after game.
You can quote me but, please, don't use my name.
I miss him, little in my arms and lap,
My innocent, my violent Anthony.

I think by now I have exhausted you.
I had to get this terror off my chest
And do appreciate your kindly eyes.
You'll meet that man and he will demonize
All of us. Our country is depressed
From guilt and violence—black man, white man, Jew.

Your eyes remind me of the Jews who went
To Mississippi with another King,
The King of Peace, the King of all our dreams.
Our leaders now are full of hate and schemes.
We've lost our souls so fast it's sickening.
You kill the King, you're ruled by Accident.

3. Ethnic Cleanser

I know you spoke to Grandma Moses who
Worked as a maid, an Aunt Jemima cook
For Sadie Schwartz or Cohen, Sadie Jew.
You'll make her bias central to your book.
Why don't you quote me on this shit?
Because this leading tough, articulate

African American will tell the truth
About the Jew who drives with his eyes shut
And aims his car directly at our youth,
 Because I've got the balls and driving butt
To take America in my direction,
Because I keep my intellectual erection.

Jews think they got the world inside their brains
—The media, top universities,
 Stock markets, banks, Congressional campaigns.
They're everywhere. They're white-faced Japanese.
Protocols of Zion tells you where they're at
Or Louis Farrakhan or Arafat.

The whole world hates them. Pick a country, man,
It tells the same bad story of the Jew.
He's greedy, violent like a Serbian.
Who started selling slaves here? Tell me who.
Those bearded, squinty people of the Book
Who'd make our Sarah Moses clean and cook.

They got no conscience as that driver showed
When he ran down that little boy, then stepped
Into an ambulance, indifferent to what he owed
To Justice. We're too kindly and inept.
We should have killed the rabbi for his crime,
That fool who makes them treat us all like slime.

They complain about our politicians
—Al Sharpton, Vernon Mason. They are gentle
Using *words*, merely rhetoricians.
We found a way to be more fundamental,
For three nights we practiced Revolution.
"Yankel's" was a model execution.

The next "accident," we'll cleanse Crown Heights.
We'll cook the Jews in ovens as before.
They're over-civilized, these bookish whites
Who own the vineyard and the vineyard store
That keeps us in this second-rate condition,
Like Palestinians, without ambition.

They keep us scapegoats like they used to be.
They hate the Muslim, Christianity.
You know they're bad for everybody's health,
These Shylocks who control this country's wealth.
There ain't no "race relations" with the Jew.
You stick that in your book. Watch what we *do*!

4. Questions

I know there is a God from what I've studied,
From what I smell in synagogues
And what I see in faces, black and white.
We're all the same in the same God's sight.
No, I'm not a "Christian martyr who's been bloodied."
I don't hate blacks, I hate their demagogues!

Some nights I think I'm better off this way.
If people talk with their hands, they won't hit
With their hands. Imagine a deaf black
(Like him) and a deaf "Jewboy out of whack"
(Like you), each struggling to have their say.
They'd feel each other's damage, every bit,

How we're two beaten people, powerless,
Expressing feelings very much alike.
What are Blues but Klezmer in a major key?
We have been friends throughout our history.
When did the oppressed start to oppress?
Why did a scholar turn into a "Kike"?

Why when we're given such gifts—our ears
For instance—can't we hear each other's virtues,
Make good assumptions, not the paranoid worst?
Why, when blessed by God, do we act cursed?
Why must we find scapegoats for our fears?
These are questions for both blacks and Jews

"To study together. *Don't be a nerd,*
My father's sneer whispers. *One-sided
Idealism only gets us burned.*
Yet '*innocence*' comes from lessons I have learned,
Which must be learned in actions, not just words.
When he calms down, he'll know I'm not *"misguided."*

Please don't shake your head! How did I become a *mensch?*
How would you be to see your son struck down
While you were helpless, beaten in the gutter?
What words of wisdom, kindness could you utter?
Like Mr. Cato, wouldn't your guts clench?
Wouldn't you feel thorns in this violent Crown

Heights? Wouldn't you be furious with *you?*
His eyes say, *Don't apologize for me.*
His eyes say, *Jews don't turn the other cheek.*
Usually we do, but we are not unique.
What's the difference between a Muslim, black, and Jew?
See: Bosnia, Soweto, Germany.

I do believe the Messiah will have to come.
Maybe to Crown Heights, if that's not arrogant.
Maybe to Harlem, Bosnia before long.
We're just thinking animals, not right or wrong
Immortals, not the "Hymie" or the "Shvartza" scum.
My father's eyes say *Shutup* but I can't

Help but be the future generation
And make good come from evil. I know it must,
Eventually. My books say so. Israel from Auschwitz.
You tell your demagogues, your hypocrites
What's stamped on every cent of this scared nation:
E Pluribus Unum, In God We Trust.

Twentieth Century

A winter evening under a John Sloan El.
Fedoras tilt in unison against the wind.
The pink neon lights of a Polish bar
Invite Grandpa in, while my son
Does pushups on the rug, and I chin
In my mother's kitchen, and my uncle
Argues he could beat Willie Pep
If Grandpa would let him turn pro. I burn
In his disappointment, forty years ago.
Now Grandpa comes brawling into the street
And, arm-weary, swaggers home on schnapps
And sits me down to watch Sugar Ray dance
Till he turn into *Counting Crows,* and my son
In my uncle's pecks flexes in the window
Where stenos in thin coats huddle against the snow.
One of them my mother, seeing my unborn face
In a taxi, hails it and rushes home.

The House We Had to Sell

This is the house we lived in, white as a bride.
Mozart is echoing the birds outside.
We're sitting at the table playing gin.
Our son is laughing every time he wins
Because he's eight, because we're all in love,
Living the future we're still dreaming of.
Spring is in the mountains, green as Oz
In the fresh-cut flowers in the crystal vase,
Mirroring the garden where the bees are thick.
Though everyone was dying, dead, or sick,
These were our uncontaminated hours,
Like bottled water sipped by scissored flowers,
Permanent in memory, sealed by the pain
That childhood ends, and we can't go home again.

Childhood's End

I need a structure to contain this pain,
A poem like a tortoise box with a silver lock,
To place it gently on the table top
And tap it with my fingertips like rain
On a garbage lid, loss loss, stop stop,
Or the tapping of a ferry against a dock,
Its passengers long departed, the decks dark,
Its pilot immobile, scared to disembark.

Poolside Mozart

Mozart slips between the fronds
Of every balletic palm,
Fingers each yellow or red
Hibiscus. Sprightly Mozart
Isn't dead. He trills,
Glissandos, double stops
Into the ears of every sun
Bather and nachos muncher
And, like the turquoise water,
Draws the fat, the slim,
The young, the aged in.
Mozart the atmosphere
Swells clouds into crescendos,
Roils tides into arpeggios.
Suspends pelicans on G-strings.
Wigless, powderless, Hispanic,
Mozart plays the Caribbean
As he plays Paris, London,
Copenhagen, Prague
Simultaneously.
Mozart digitized
Is mathematics musicalized,
An orderly surprise,
Like this teenage girl,
Having swallowed too much water,
Spits a perfect cone of spray,
Each drop a solid grace note.

Blue Caribbean Picnic

To a young painter

Closing your eyes to sun, you merely mock
These guests—small children dressed in turtle shells
Of life vests, blond hair festooned in dreadlocks,
Kayaking or snorkling; and *demoiselles*
From "Oshkosh or Pawcatuck" chalking sun block
Where they want pubescent boys to fix their gaze;
And fathers dangling guppies from the dock,
And mothers nibbling chicken in mayonnaise.
But Cezanne, Renoir, Maurice Prendergast
Would celebrate their flesh-tones, and their shapes
Anchored in composition with these yachts,
Would make brushstrokes of blue sail covers, dots
Of blue bathing suits, blue shadows of masts,
And edible blue curlicues of grapes.

Creation

The soul must be rinsed in time
Where Sufis and Baptists stand
With washerwomen bringing shirts
Patterned like mandalas of sand

That monks make and destroy.
Once we stood on a bank,
Shadowless beside a river,
While over us passed a clank

Of geese, invisible and unborn,
Our feathers linnet-white,
We bathed what we must mourn
In waves of broken light.

I write this in the middle of the night,
One finger a moonlit taper
Burning like an acolyte
In a passion of pen and paper.

BIOGRAPHICAL NOTE

Frederick Feirstein has had nine previous books of poems published, seven by Story Line and the Quarterly Review of Literature. He has been the recipient of a Guggenheim Fellowship, the Poetry Society of America's John Masefield Award, and England's Arvon Prize. Twelve of his plays have been produced. Three are musical dramas, his lyrics deriving from his poetry. His third, *Uprising*, will be done as a film. He made his living writing film and television while he trained as a psychoanalyst. He is in private practice in New York City and on the faculty of the National Psychological Association for Psychoanalysis. His autobiography is in the Contemporary Authors Autobiography Series and his biography in the Dictionary of Literary Biography.

www.ingramcontent.com/pod-product-compliance
Lightning Source LLC
Chambersburg PA
CBHW030856170426
43193CB00009BA/632